A French GI
at Omaha Beach

Dedication

To Françoise, Yetta, Paul, Marcel and Simon

*For the GI's great-grandchildren Mila, Tom, Jules, Sasha,
Nicholas and their cousins and friends, Gabriel, Magdalena,
Nathanaël, Henri, Lula, Yarol, Lena, Zoe, Joshua, Léo, Côme,
April, Paul, Joseph, Eléonore, Ladislas, Côme, Eva, Ethan,
Adrien, Mia, Yanis, Naël, Ellie, Patrick, William, Hadrien,
Alice, Mila, Maxime, Ulysse, Charlotte and Romane.*

A French GI
at Omaha Beach

Caroline Jolivet

Pen & Sword
MILITARY
AN IMPRINT OF PEN & SWORD BOOKS LTD.
YORKSHIRE - PHILADELPHIA

First published by Editions Ouest-France in 2012 as
Bernard Dargols, un GI français à Omaha Beach

First published in Great Britain in 2018 by
Pen & Sword Military
An imprint of
Pen & Sword Books Ltd
Yorkshire - Philadelphia

ISBN 978 1 52673 045 9

A CIP catalogue record for this book is available from the British Library.

Printed and bound in England
By TJ International Ltd.

Pen & Sword Books Ltd incorporates the Imprints of Pen & Sword Books Archaeology, Atlas, Aviation, Battleground, Discovery, Family History, History, Maritime, Military, Naval, Politics, Railways, Select, Transport, True Crime, Fiction, Frontline Books, Leo Cooper, Praetorian Press, Seaforth Publishing, Wharncliffe and White Owl.

For a complete list of Pen & Sword titles please contact

PEN & SWORD BOOKS LIMITED
47 Church Street, Barnsley, South Yorkshire, S70 2AS, England
E-mail: enquiries@pen-and-sword.co.uk
Website: www.pen-and-sword.co.uk

or

PEN AND SWORD BOOKS
1950 Lawrence Rd, Havertown, PA 19083, USA
E-mail: Uspen-and-sword@casematepublishers.com
Website: www.penandswordbooks.com

Contents

Bernard Dargols has the greatness of the heroes of the night. Like them he has learned to do great things in silence. There is no need for him to flaunt, he simply is. He is here and catches all the light, he talks and one listens, he stays quiet, but continues to talk. Still, one would have to learn to hear this peacefully obstinate silence... And from this warm smile exudes a joie de vivre, *his inner flame, which will not be snuffed out. Like the men and women who worked in darkness and mystery for our greatest liberty, he is for me the shadow of the wind...*

José Manuel Lamarque, *France Inter*
[French public radio] journalist

Foreword

Above all, as I recount my grandfather's life in this book, my hope is to carry his message loud and clear. By passing on his story, his anecdotes, and by answering my countless questions, he passed on his duty never to forget to me. This is a story which involves far more than my family.

When I became a mother, my grandmother, who so regrets not having asked her parents enough questions, paved the way for mine. For me it wasn't too late and I am grateful for the chance I was given to record my grandfather's account of his participation in one of the twentieth century's most significant events.

When the opportunity arose in 2005 I travelled with my grandparents and a small video camera to the place where it all started for them; New York City. They took me to where they met, lived, and got married. But it took a while longer to touch on the subject of my grandfather's landing at Omaha Beach in 1944. It wasn't easy to unearth the close secrets of someone who, to better protect us from them, chose to bury them deep down for a very long time.

My grandparents used the medium of cinema to convey their story to us. As a family ritual, my parents and grandparents took my brother Romain and me to the movies to see *Europa, Europa, Schindler's List* and *Saving Private Ryan*. Despite my grandfather's knack of resorting to humour to hide his feelings, he was moved to tears and we in turn were deeply moved. He told us, 'I've never seen a movie that so accurately captured what I lived [through].' Understanding dawned on us for the first time. And who could be better than Tom Hanks to introduce us to his story?

With his jolly demeanour, my grandfather, 'Daddy', is our role model, a man less interested in himself than others. How would life be today if on that day in June 1944 he and his friends hadn't proved themselves so brave and selfless, and indeed, for some, laid down their lives, in order to give us our freedom?

Unravelling his story requires reading between his many punch lines: a body armour of jokes crafted to play down his hardships and the enduring mark they left on him. Although I'm older than he was when he enrolled in the US Army, I do wonder if I would have had the courage he summoned to overcome his fear. He who, at ninety-seven years of age, continues to demonstrate against extreme "-isms" of all kinds and to defend the causes he holds dear, frequently cautions me: 'it could happen again. Be on the alert at all times. The horrors of the war were committed by educated people, who did so of their own willpower.'[1]

I witnessed many interviews he has given since the 50th anniversary of D-Day, during which I discovered the vulnerability which took him years to mend. His silences and the tears he held back spoke for themselves; they prompted me to become his penman or the 'witness bearer' recounting his story, and to escort him along his 'journey of remembrance.'[2] Between 2012, when this book was first published in French, and 2017, I myself had to face tragic events. Another kind of war which targets us all now: terrorism. How I wish my grandparents hadn't had to go through even more by losing a man they considered just as another of their own grandchild, my beloved and loving husband, Christophe. My grandfather's story, to which I had tried to remain true to by carefully choosing each of his words, suddenly echoed violently in my new reality: the horror, the powerlessness and the need to rise and act were once more back in our lives. More than ever I now understood Elie Wiesel's words: 'Beyond laughter is the truth... We laugh in order not to cry. We also tell not to cry, we transmit not to cry.'[3]

Introduction

Forty years of silence. That seems like a long time but it was the time I needed to find the words to tell my story. My cousin David Badache, an Auschwitz survivor, couldn't find the words either, which is probably why we were so close: having at one point in our lives experienced something that cannot be told because words seem not to measure up to reality. Who should I have talked to? To my wife Françoise; to my three children whom I wanted to raise as far removed from my war years as I could? I chose not to tell them. To my brothers Marcel and Simon who had endured the exodus from occupied France, and the state of war? We wrote to each other very often during that period, but after the Liberation we never broached the subject, as if to forget and stop wondering why we'd survived when so many others had perished. Or maybe just for the sake of self-preservation and living in peace?

I only started answering questions during the celebration of D-Day's 40th anniversary. Journalists, curious to know my story, asked me the very questions which my family, eager to protect me, hadn't dared to. Hadn't I myself spared my grandfather from any such questions concerning the internment in Drancy which he'd survived? Now that I'm ninety-seven, the duty to carry the torch really nags me more than ever. Each morning as I shave I recognize my physical decline, but my heart is still that of an eighteen-year-old. It is the heart of a kid who left France for New York in 1938 and only returned six years later as an American GI among thousands of brothers in arms who landed at Omaha Beach to carry out their duty.

CHAPTER 1

A Frenchie in New York

I was born in Paris on 5 May 1920, to a Russian father and an English mother. We lived in the heart of Paris, near the Place des Vosges. My father, Paul Dargols, a mechanical engineer, had moved to France at the age of eighteen and settled in the garment district to run a small sewing machine store. He'd left Russia with his family in 1913 to escape the pogroms. After fleeing Russia, his family scattered to the winds, to Argentina, England and Australia, but my father's parents chose Paris. Although none spoke a word of French when they arrived, brothers and sisters challenged each other to be the first to speak it fluently. A few years later Paul met and married my mother, Yetta Bloom, whose Lithuanian parents had immigrated to England. Every Thursday afternoon, I would visit my maternal grandparents in the 11th arrondissement of Paris. They lived in a tiny studio apartment with toilets and washroom on the landing, but their modest circumstances did not prevent them from being kind and generous. Grand-Father Bloom was a cabinetmaker and crafted propellers for the French Air Force during the First World War. He had a great sense of deadpan humour, and taught me many things, especially chess.

With my mother's help, my father's business grew fast, the small shop gradually turning into an important store with a showroom. My father quickly attracted many customers. He became the exclusive representative in France, Belgium and the colonies and sole importer of industrial sewing machines from

Bernard's parents, Yetta Bloom and Paul Dargols. Paris, 1920s. (Dargols Family Archive)

The Dargols' sewing machines store. 8 rue des Francs-Bourgeois, Paris, 3ʳᵈ arrondissement. (Dargols Family Archive)

three American factories based in New York City, in Cincinnati, Ohio, and in New Jersey.

At home, a good-humoured family spirit prevailed. My maternal grandparents moved in with us and my paternal grandparents visited us often. All spoke Yiddish or English. As for my parents, they insisted on speaking French exclusively with my two younger brothers, Simon and Marcel, and me. Respect and non-violence were the key to our secular education.

I attended l'Ecole Turgot [a local public school] where I excelled above all in English, thanks to my mother and Mr Soulas, an excellent teacher and a surprising Fred Astaire look-alike. I always expected him to hop and tap dance on his desk.

My father had great expectations for me, the eldest of his three sons. He wanted me to take over his business in the future.

I was a rather good student, but very shy. My father was quite the opposite, a man with a strong personality. To help me overcome my shyness, he had me take boxing lessons from a professional, not to learn attack—being non-violent by nature—but to know how to defend myself in life. It was George Papin, a 1920 French championship winner, who made me love not boxing but physical exercise. Little did I know at the time how useful this would turn out to be. Thanks to him I acquired a certain authority and learned to cope with my shyness.

***

During a visit to the United States in the late 1930s, my father organized a year-long internship with the three American manufacturers we represented in Paris. In the factories, I would learn a trade and would then be free to take off by myself. Upon returning from his transatlantic trip, and just as I'd failed the entrance to the Arts et Métiers [a top engineering school], he announced: 'You're going to the States. I've arranged everything. At least when you replace me it won't be said that it's because you're the boss's son.'

I was beside myself with joy! Like all French kids my age, I dreamed of discovering America, which I knew only through movies, books and music. My brothers and I lapped up everything American, such as the music of Benny Goodman, Frank Sinatra, Ella Fitzgerald, Fred Astaire, Duke Ellington, Glenn Miller and Louis Armstrong, among others.

So, in December 1938, when I was eighteen, I sailed off for New York from Le Havre on the steamship *Paris*. Today I can only imagine my mother's heartache when she saw me leave on my own. As for me, I was at once elated and scared by my big step into the unknown. The crossing lasted around ten days. I then realized that, unlike many fellow passengers, I wasn't in the least bit sea-sick.

***

From left to right: Paul, Yetta, Bernard and in the foreground Marcel and Simon. Paris, 1935. (Dargols Family Archive)

From left to right: Bernard, Marcel and Simon Dargols. Paris, 1938. (Dargols Family Archive)

A manager of the *Consolidated* factory, where I was to start working, was waiting for me in New York. I was overwhelmed by the gigantic proportions of the city which I fell in love with immediately. The next day, I went to the corner of 25th Street and Broadway, a few steps away from the Flatiron Building. The workers, all older than me, adopted the little 'Frenchie' right away. They took me to sports clubs. Everything was possible for an 18-year-old in New York. Over there, at that age, you could already run a business, which was inconceivable in France at the time and difficult to this day. At first my English accent tended to the English variety, but I quickly became a master of New York slang. My new friends all dreamed of going to France where they thought life was more easygoing. While shops in Paris closed for two hours for lunch, factories and stores stayed open in New York. We had a 35-minute-break during which I would devour sandwiches of corned beef or pastrami on rye bread with pickles, or on squares of toasted white bread, covered with cream cheese and jelly, washed down with refills of weak coffee served in paper cups.

Distant relatives of my mother in Brooklyn, the Sandlers, put me up at first, before I moved to Manhattan, on Lexington and 82nd Street. Later, I lived in a studio on 108th Street. On weekends, I would help my cousin Philip in his clothing store in Brooklyn, where I kept an eye out for shoplifters. In the evenings, we would watch movies at the Paramount, especially when an orchestra was scheduled to play during the show.

Saturday, 17 December 1938, New York

I saw the Empire State Building today. It is higher than the Eiffel Tower. Couldn't see the top of it as it was lost in the haze. It's freezing out there. Everything is going well at work.

Saturday, 24 December 1938, New York

I spent Christmas at Milton's, in his picture-perfect house a few miles away from New York. As it was snowing outside, the lights filtering through the curtains looked just like a photo by Alfred Stieglitz. It was unforgettable.

Saturday, 31 December 1938, New York

Phil and I went to Times Square tonight. The joy, this infernal noise, people going crazy and wild, the endless rush, dazzling lights: I'll never forget the last day of 1938.

But this easygoing life ended on 3 September 1939. On 1 September 1939, Germany's invasion of Poland triggered the declaration of war on Germany by Britain and France, which I learned about while at work. I was working in the workshop when I heard on the radio that France and Britain had declared war on Germany. Hitler had annexed Austria by referendum and in turn conquered Czechoslovakia, Poland, Denmark, Norway, the Netherlands, Luxembourg and Belgium. After each victory, he would claim that no other country had his eye but would nonetheless maintain that Germany needed more vital space (*Lebensraum*). Nothing seemed to stop the dangerous dictator whose yearning to rule the world ("Deutschland über alles") and impose his ideology founded on the superiority of the German "race" was obvious. On 1 September 1939, Poland's invasion triggered the declaration of war on Germany by Britain and France.

Monday, 4 September 1939, New York

All the programs were interrupted by flash bulletins. The Allies have not taken any measures yet. I haven't heard anything from Papa, he might have to go to war?

The SS Athenia, a British ship going to the USA was struck and sunk. 200 dead out of 1400. Presumed guilty: a German U-boat.

I'm sure Maman will stay in Paris instead of being evacuated.

I expect to have to go back to Paris anytime soon.

Tuesday, 26 September 1939, New York

Once again today, like yesterday, no mail.

Kids run in the streets selling newspaper extras but I've learned that the size of the headlines has nothing to do with the truth!

During several months after the declaration of war we still hoped for a political agreement, to no avail. The imminence of war was palpable. The "phony war," as it was referred to, was a war without combat, a strange period which ended in June 1940 with France's defeat and the signing of an armistice with Nazi Germany by Pétain.

I was very worried for my family and friends in France. My two younger brothers, my parents, my four grandparents were all in Paris; my internship was coming to an end and I was meant to join them no more than a few months later. From the onset of war, mail had become scarce and was censored by the Germans. We were used to writing regularly to each other, and now I had little news from them.

Monday, 4 October 1939, New York

Headlines are all about the Baseball World series between the Yankees and Cincinnati.

Friday, 6 October 1939, New York

Hitler spoke for more than an hour proposing an armistice (including Germany recovering its former colonies) but the kind of Peace he offers seems unacceptable to the Allies. In spite of Hitler's threat of a bloody war and major destructions, they are staying put and will most certainly continue fighting.

Wednesday, 11 October 1939, New York

Just heard that Russia and Britain signed a trade agreement!

Chamberlain is expected to talk tomorrow.

No letter from Paris since 29 September.

Sunday, 15 October 1939, New York

I've been in the US for ten months.

I wish I could celebrate my twentieth birthday in Paris at peace.

In school, my brothers were given gas masks. Once a week sirens would blast throughout Paris for emergency drills. In October 1939, the Diderot [public] school, where 15-year-old Marcel studied, was transferred to Vierzon [some 350 kilometres south of Paris]. Young Jews from Germany, who had fled their country, arrived in 14-year-old Simon's class in Boulogne Billancourt [a Parisian suburb]. The school was ultimately closed in June 1940.

My father, conditioned by his Russian past, was aware of the danger and could sense that the situation was bound to go wrong.

***

The French authorities contacted me in May 1940, the month I turned twenty. I received a letter ordering me to come to the French Consulate on 5th Avenue for my *conseil de révision* [draft board examination], like any 20-year-old Frenchman who was to be conscripted. After a cursory examination, the doctor pronounced me 'fit for [military] service' and said: 'wait for us to call you, we will repatriate you to France so you can carry out your military duty.' My American friends were optimistic; the French Army was deemed one of the world's best. However, despite its reputation, only six weeks after my appointment we learned that France had been invaded by the Germans. The defeat of France, beaten and occupied within a few weeks by the German troops in June 1940, came as a major shock.

In New York, I had more information on the situation in Paris than my family. From May 1940 to May 1942 the American ambassador appointed by President Roosevelt, Admiral Leahy, stayed in Vichy and observed the regime headed by Pétain. Whereas the French press and radio were censored by the German authorities, American journalists were allowed to cover the whole country, including the occupied zones, until the end of 1941. Therefore, we in the United States were more informed than the French themselves. I remember the slogan of the time, broadcast from London, 'Radio Paris ment, Radio Paris ment, Radio Paris est Allemand.' ['Radio Paris is lying, Radio Paris is lying, Radio Paris is German'] The news broadcast by the American press confirmed the French's enslavement by Germany: in October 1940, Pétain shook Hitler's hand, thereby announcing the 'collaboration policy' between France and Nazi Germany. From then onward it became obvious to me that, even if ordered by the Consulate to return to France, I would disobey. I could never join Pétain's Army.

Given the tragic turn of events, I met with De Gaulle's representative in New York. Colonel De Manziarly, a disabled war veteran with a slight limp, gracefully received me in his New York office, near 5th Avenue. He was in charge of military enlistments. I was thinking about joining the *Forces Françaises Libres*. [Free French Forces]. He inquired about my studies, my work, my private life. After our meeting, he explained that, if I enlisted with the Gaullist Army, he would see to my transfer to London where I would immediately be made an officer. At the time, the difference between a commissioned and non-commissioned officer, and a private, was quite beyond me. If he offered me a high rank straight away this was because *France Libre* [Free France] lacked soldiers, officers, weapons, vehicles, uniforms and relied on the Americans and British for everything. The United States became the Allied armies' arsenal. In 1940 Roosevelt said: 'We must be the great arsenal of democracy'.[4] American industry as a whole was mobilized: Remington typewriters manufactured machine guns, Willys and Ford, jeeps, General Motors, trucks, and Chrysler, tanks.

Thanks to their assembly lines Americans could in ten hours build a Bofors canon, whose patent they had brought from Sweden who took twenty times longer to make the same weapon.

Colonel De Manziarly told me: 'Think it over and then come back.'

For my workshop colleagues, who knew about the meeting, there was no doubt that the United States would not stay out of the conflict for long. The peacetime draft had just begun in September 1940: 'Join us in the US Army'. I remained undecided. I knew little about De Gaulle except that he'd been France's Secretary of State for War for a short time and that he did not get on well with Churchill or Roosevelt. I preferred waiting a few months to see if the United States joined the war, as we anticipated it would.

At twenty-one, the legal age to do so, I decided to enrol in the US military. It seemed to me that speaking French, I would be most useful to the battle against the armies occupying France with the US Army. I went to the recruiting center. I was told: 'We'll call you'. In hindsight, I am convinced I made the right choice.

***

Being far from my family and friends started to weigh on me. My letters remained unanswered. When several months later, stuck in New York City, I learned of the terrible events that affected them so violently, I felt helpless.

At the time of the German invasion in May 1940, Marcel was still in Vierzon with his school. My parents sent Simon to a safe place with friends, sewing machine suppliers near Cholet [around 350 kilometres south-west of Paris]. My father, concerned about his sons, decided to join them in the free zone—at the time, France was divided into three zones: to the north of the Loire valley, an entirely occupied zone; south of the river, the zone known as *libre* [free], governed by Pétain in Vichy; and lastly, the seldom mentioned so-called *zone interdite* [no-go zone], a coastal fringe a few kilometres wide, running all along the Atlantic up to Belgium. Its access was forbidden to all except residents. Later, the German Todt organization constructed the 'Atlantic Wall' on this coastal fringe: they laid out landmines and obstacles and built blockhouses on the beaches and inland, all in an effort to discourage a potential landing of the Allies.

Despite my father's urging, my mother refused to leave my elderly grandparents alone in Paris. She decided to stay on.

She wrote me a letter:

Paris, 11 June 1940

My dear Bernard,

In spite of the Italians, we still have hope. Don't worry about us. We have enough time to be safe and sound. Simon is for now in Lencloître in the Vienne [French department]. As for Marcel, he's in Vierzon. I hope everything will be alright. I'm sorry I cannot keep you warm when you are cold. Will we someday be reunited? Good bye my darling, if we've at least managed to keep you safe, I'll always be happy and I only regret not having been able to better reassure you.

Then, a letter from Marcel reached me in June 1940:

Vierzon, 14 June 1940

My school was ordered to evacuate to the South. Maman tells me to stay in Vierzon and to wait for Papa to come get me. We will join Simon in Cholet. The situation here is impressive: hundreds and hundreds of cars filled with refugees have turned up from Paris. Railroads are overworked, trains transporting machines from Parisian factories follow each other barely 20 meters apart! All these families coming from the North, packed in their cars, with boxes and suitcases on the roof, who wait for hours for a few litres of fuel to continue their trip. What a mess, it's incredible!

My father told me what followed in another letter:

When we arrived in Cholet, Simon wasn't there. He had left for Condom with our friends to outrun the Germans' fast progress. We did the same, but I had no fuel left. We had to wait three days and finally obtained half a litre. Marcel and I slept and ate in the car.

I managed to drive about 10 kilometres and then we stopped in a small village. The next day, the Italian air force bombed and sprayed the surroundings with bullets. Machine gun bullets fell just a few meters from us. We were overwhelmed by fear.

I then decided to leave everything on the spot with an innkeeper: the car and all the goods I'd taken with me. Marcel and I left on foot with a little suitcase, avoiding the main road and Poitiers. With a small map, we tried to go straight to the South by taking side-roads. We neither ate nor slept but we had to keep going because the Germans were very close. We went as fast as we could. We were afraid of meeting the Germans at every crossroads. But after 15 kilometres our feet were very sore: each step felt like torture. Aeroplanes flew overhead: we dared not look up, but scrambled into the ditches along the road, flat on our stomach.

He continued his account: *Fortunately, we escaped unhurt. Step by step and painstakingly we travelled 40 kilometres, at the end of which we found a hotel in Lencloître where we were allowed some sleep. It was my birthday—44 years. The next day, we had to set off again on foot because the enemy was moving too fast and we had to keep going at all costs despite the heat, blisters and injuries. I had a stick in hand and we had to rest every few kilometres. We're doing relatively well now. We're staying in a hotel-restaurant and don't need to sleep on straw any more. Every day we go fishing. Communications are severed. As a result, I need to wait some 10 to 15 days to return to Paris because we're in the non-occupied zone. I have sent Maman letter upon letter but of course haven't had an answer as the postal services aren't working. In short, I can't give you news from Paris, I know nothing. Maman will send you a telegram and me too when I reach Paris. These are some unpleasant details of our flight, and I hope that will be the end of it. Concerning the future, the situation isn't brilliant and above all uncertain. In my mind, vague ideas of leaving for the States or elsewhere. But I've decided to wait and see if the "racial" laws will pass or not. If they do, then we will remain in the non-occupied zone or we will take a boat to go further away.*

Ultimately, after over a month in the free zone my father asked for an Ausweiss to return to the occupied zone, which he easily obtained. Like many French people in July 1940 he thought the situation had calmed down and that they could return to Paris.

Unfortunately, my father had it right about the anti-Semitic laws and they were adopted by Pétain in October 1940, wreaking havoc on the lives of my family and friends who had stayed in Paris. Their situation quickly became unbearable. The racial laws enforced in the northern part of France banned Jews from many trades and required that they report themselves to the police. No matter what, whether practising Jews or not, baptized or not. A single Jewish member three generations back was enough for a whole family to be required to report. If one failed to do so, others would most certainly take it upon themselves to correct that mistake, as shown by the millions of anonymous denunciation letters sent during the war.

Tuesday, 8 October 1940 New York

London is enduring its most terrible raid to this day.

US citizens living in the Far East have been strongly advised by State Department to come back. The US—Japan War will soon be upon us.

In France, the anti-Semitic press, *La Gerbe, Je Suis Partout, Le Pilori*, went wild. Paris was overrun by pro-Nazi pamphlets and posters. The police searched homes to find anti-Nazi pamphlets, ID checks proliferated, and Jews, communists, Gaullists, gypsies and Freemasons were routinely arrested. The Gestapo even came to the store, asked who was Jewish and snatched away several employees. Faced with these arrests my father was helpless, and was forced to give up his shop and had to wait for an assigned non-Jewish manager to replace him. A signboard, 'Jewish business', was on display on the store front.

In Paris, my family held their breath and lived in fear. In February 1941, after his store was requisitioned, my father wrote to me:

Don't worry, I will handle this for the best. I hope to liquidate the store soon and set off again for the free zone and if possible America or England. You know what is happening here through the newspapers and radio. Unfortunately, everything is true and we cheer up by listening to the B.B.C. from London, Boston USA or even Columbia. It's very comforting for us over here. I would like to be in America because this situation is becoming intolerable for any human being. Don't worry, stay in America and soon we will breathe freely and the sun will shine for everyone again.

***

After this letter, I had no news from France for seven long months.

My concern was growing: I didn't know if my family was safe. Working and writing letters which were never answered were my only way to stave off anxiety. I was still waiting for a call from the army which wouldn't come, and my situation as an intern was becoming precarious. I couldn't, however, get a job with a limited time internship visa.

Saturday, 1 February 1941, New York

I still feel powerless to do anything for my family and friends in Paris.

Secretary of the Navy Knox says he is concerned by how long it will take for the American help to get there. Maybe too late. I went to the British consulate to get information about enrolling. But they only need youngsters for the Navy.

In Paris, tipped off by a policeman friend and fishing companion of my father, my brothers destroyed all magazines and documents in English and records by Anglo-American artists as well as the letters I wrote them. Later, Marcel told me:

…The Germans visited apartments. We lived in a permanent state of alarm. During the month of July, when the temperature was stifling, we had to take turns at the kitchen stoves, poking the piles of papers which weren't burning fast enough. In that way, we burned many newspapers from New York, English and American periodicals and even London maps you'd brought back when you were over there on vacation. We had gathered in a file all the letters we had received from you since you'd left for New York. And it was with great reluctance that we had to burn it, as well as an enormous quantity of letters from the family. In the kitchen, the heat was such that the atmosphere was as suffocating as a furnace.

A few days later, my father, on his way to Ballancourt, some 60 kilometres from Paris, where he used to go fishing every weekend, called my mother from close to the Bastille train station. Before his eyes the police were checking IDs and arresting Jews. He was on the 4th arrondissement side of Boulevard Beaumarchais. The round up was in the 11th arrondissement, on the pavement across the street. Marcel and Simon needed to hide as quickly as possible. My mother hung up. Simon and Marcel ran to take shelter in the store's basement.

Simon explained:

As the store remained closed for a few days, Marcel and I stayed in the basement all day long and slept there. Maman would bring us food through the back door. During moments of respite we'd go home, always on the alert, and the doorbell ringing was enough to make us leap up. Zorick, our public accountant's son, wasn't as lucky as we were, and at 7 one morning the Gestapo dragged him out of bed to an internment camp.

This time, the Gestapo didn't go that far. Once the calm returned, my brothers emerged from their hideout. Weeks of fear were starting for them. Dreading capture, they never left the apartment. What would have happened if my father had taken the other pavement?

During the summer of 1941, our neighbour Madame Godard knocked on our door one night: 'The Germans are searching all the houses. Tell your children to hide, fast!' Marcel's letter went on:

The Nazis encircled the Rue des Francs-bourgeois. At 4 am, Maman woke us up, Simon and I. Fortunately Papa was in Ballancourt. At full speed, we pulled on our trousers. We took the rest of our clothes and ran out like crazy and hid in the little attic bedrooms. Meanwhile Maman made our beds. At around 6 am, Maman came to tell us that, one by one, houses in the 4th arrondissement (across the street) were being searched for weapons and anti-Nazi pamphlets. The search was ongoing. Locked doors were forced open and everything was inspected, even the chimney pipes. From that day onward, we were afraid not only of going outside, but also of staying home! We didn't know if the next day our arrondissement might be surrounded.

During the round-up in the 3rd arrondissement, Simon and Marcel, from the small window of the attic room where our grandparents slept, watched as some men of the "new order," wearing black armbands, drew in from right and left of the street and arrested our uncle Salomon. These weren't Germans but well and truly the French police. Salomon came to see us every other day. Unlike Marcel and Simon who holed up in the apartment, he refused to give in to fear and hide as he had a few years prior in Odessa. He said it wasn't in his nature. We never saw him again. Later we learned that he had been deported to

Auschwitz, and that subsequently, the whole 11th arrondissement was surrounded. The police arrested 8,000 Jews and sent them to the death camps.

After these events, and for his children's sake, my father resolved to leave, aware of the imminent danger of staying in the occupied zone. Considering his active role in the LICA,[5] an organization fighting against anti-Semitism, his arrest was almost inevitable. He was an easy target; he had no choice but to leave. Moreover, his store having been confiscated, he couldn't work and provide for his family. Fear was everybody's daily lot. The arrest of his brother and several friends finally decided him to go. Once again, my mother faced the dilemma of whether to leave with her sons and husband or to stay with and care for her aging and ailing parents and in-laws. Women and elderly people were not as yet threatened, so she chose to stay in Paris.

***

My parents knew of a people smuggler who had helped some friends' children get to the free zone. They agreed that they would leave on 18 September 1941. The night before, the family gathered for one last dinner. Marcel, overcome with emotion, could not eat. They took a last family picture before their departure.

The following day, my mother accompanied my brothers to the Gare d'Austerlitz [southbound train station]. On the way, she handed over the agreed amount to the smuggler and Simon and Marcel were indeed taken across the line of demarcation from where they carried on to Marseilles without being threatened by the police. The city had become a hub for refugees seeking to go abroad. My father joined them by train a few days later after arranging to have the store taken over by a French rival in order to protect his business. In the free zone, they were helped by sewing machine retailers, members of the trade union association of which my father was the secretary.

My father was living his second forced departure since birth: as a young man, he had fled Russia when the Cossacks had requisitioned the family grocery store because his father was

Back row (L to R): Marcel, Golda Viesben, Linka Veisben and Yetta Bloom, Bernard's mother. Front row: Bernard's maternal grandparents. Photograph taken the family apartment in Paris, 12 September 1941. (Dargols Family Archive)

Jewish. They had left my unrelenting grandfather no choice: 'If you continue to refuse, we will get your grocery for nothing.' Threatened with death, my father, his parents and six brothers and sisters fled Russia and headed towards France, by foot or cart. After crossing the river Dniestr, they would be safe. My father's young brother Marcel once recounted this episode in tears. During the flight, he had been left alone on the Russian side of the river. Just eleven years old at the time he was terrified but, fortunately, his parents had realized the mishap and turned back to fetch him and then carried on. In Paris, the family settled in Passage Bafroi, in the 11th arrondissement. They didn't know anyone, but at last they were free. In France, the country of human rights where his family had chosen to take shelter to live in freedom, my father was reliving the same nightmare: anti-Semitic laws, and once again the family store requisitioned. It was time to go.

***

After they left, the Gestapo returned to the apartment many times, asking where we were, Simon, Marcel, my father and I. 'Tell them to come see us when they come back.' In Marseilles, my father started the bureaucratic process to leave the country by boat, hoping to join me in New York. Meanwhile, Simon was arrested by the French Milice [paramilitary force fighting the Resistance] because his ID papers weren't in order. After much bargaining and thanks to the help of HICEM, an organization helping Jews to escape the country, he was released. A pretext was found by the same stubborn guy to arrest him a second time. Luckily, someone from the Milice once again let him go.

A cable sent on 31 October 1941 by Paul Dargols, in Marseilles, to his son
Bernard in New York, replying to a previous cable from Bernard on
27 September 1941: 'TAKING CARE OF THE PAPERS AND TICKETS TO
GET YOU IN CUBA AS SOON AS POSSIBLE...' (Dargols Family Archive)

Simon described to me their journey:

Marseilles, Monday, 24 November 1941

Now that we have our visas and passports, Papa went to the HICEM to get our names on the passengers list for next departure. We might leave in a couple of weeks. Papa said we have to rush to Portugal if we don't want to be stuck here. This afternoon the three of us went to the Alcazar cinema on Belsunce drive to see "Alerte en mer"

Marseilles, Wednesday, 3 December 1941

The newspapers announced measures taken against the Jews in the non-occupied zone and the arrest of Jews who would not have ID papers or affidavits.

Marseilles, Monday, 8 December 1941

Japan bombed Pearl Harbor without any warning. The United States entered the War. This is not going to ease our trip to Cuba as the American consul has stopped delivering visas.

We received a letter from Maman: The Gestapo came home for Grandma and Grandpa Bloom. Fortunately, they didn't get arrested.

After almost three months in Marseilles and through HICEM, my father and brothers obtained the affidavits they needed to prove that they wouldn't become a financial burden for Cuba, and were allowed aboard the S.S. *Chanzy*. They transited first by Oran, then Casablanca, before taking yet another boat, the *Guinee*, which led them to Cuba via Bermuda. Their trip lasted seventeen days and was extremely difficult, but was never attacked. Once aboard, they felt safe. Upon arriving in Havana in January 1942, they were interrogated at length by the FBI. Once cleared, and free at last, they settled in a hotel. A few weeks later, they learned that aboard the ship, among the 174 Jewish refugees, was a Nazi spy named Luning. He was arrested by the

From left to right: Simon, Paul and Marcel Dargols. Marseilles, October 1941. (Dargols Family Archive)

FBI and executed. Maybe this accounted for their never being attacked by an enemy ship during the long crossing?

Entering the United States from Cuba proved longer than expected. The deposit requested for a temporary visa application was very high.

***

Marcel Dargols. Marseilles, October 1941. (Dargols Family Archive)

My bosses from the factory immediately agreed to vouch for my father and to lend him the $1,500 he needed to obtain his and my brothers' entry permits to the United States: it was only the beginning of a complicated administrative procedure. As soon as he could, my father made it a point of honour to pay back, penny by penny, this considerable amount.

Little by little, the young men on 25th Street where I worked were all called to arms. Sewing machine manufacturers were starting to be short on manpower. I was still an intern with Consolidated, but other factories were offering me two or three times my salary. But, despite my extreme financial situation, I didn't want to jeopardize my family's entry into the United States by leaving Consolidated. I needed to be patient. All I could do as I waited to be drafted was to work and write. I would send my letters to Angel, a friend in Périgueux, in the non-occupied zone, and he would deliver them to my family, thus bypassing censorship.

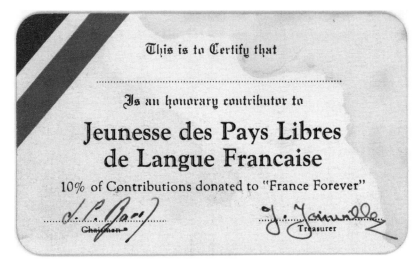

*Membership card for the Jeunesse France Libre (Free France Youth)
association.* (Dargols Family Archive)

After my factory hours, during which I continued to work
on industrial sewing machines—the machines sewing buttons,
buttonholes, those over-sewing, the so-called invisible stitch
machines, and those designed to make everything, from shoes to
military caps, from shirts to boxer shorts or uniforms—I would
go to the *Jeunesse France Libre* organization [Free France Youth
organization] which I had founded with my friend Maurice
Shire.

Our goal was to bring together the anti-Pétain Francophone
people of New York. We organized ping-pong tournaments,
conferences and dances, and collected funds for France Forever,
a large US based Gaullist organization. We were roughly a
hundred Francophone members, 19 years old on average, and,
coming from Belgium, France or Switzerland, some members
of our families were always in Europe. Left-wing or right-wing,
we all had a common goal: to support Gaullist France and, in
our modest way, help win the war. In order to draw attention
to the organization, I had written a letter which was published
in the 'Letters to the Editor' section of the *New York Times* on
4 January 1943, using the pen-name Bernard Darville, to avoid
putting my family in France at risk. 'We shall never see the same

Paris or the same France we left. But none of us in Jeunesse France Libre want to see it the same. We want to see a better France, a better world - and we shall put the spirit of our youth to attain this goal.'

During a *Jeunesse France Libre* gathering, I met Françoise, who was born in France and lived in New York with her parents.

Françoise's father, Jean Benoit-Lévy, was a well-known film producer and director banned from the film industry in France by the anti-Semitic laws.

In August 1941, he was in the small village of Montflanquin where he and his family had taken refuge in the free zone, when the Rockefeller Foundation in New York offered him a chair in cinema at the New School for Social Research. At first, convinced that the war wasn't going to last, he rejected the idea of leaving the country. A World War I veteran, awarded the *Croix de guerre* [Cross of War, a French military decoration], he believed he had nothing to fear. He was a 'good Frenchman' who had fought for his country. Many

French Youth United

To the Editor of The New York Times:

Many of the letters you have printed lately concerned France. None, however, dealt with the thoughts or opinions of the exiled youth of France in this city.

Two months ago a club was started under the name of Jeunesse France Libre. It counts, so far, about 100 boys and girls; their average age is 19. All members came from France or Belgium very recently. All left friends over there and many still have relatives or parents abroad.

In Jeunesse France Libre, ex-leftists and ex-rightists all are united with one common aim—help, in our humble way, to win the war.

Our activities consist mainly in bringing the French-speaking youth together. By giving dances, ping-pong parties or gathering in talk sessions we raise money which is to be given to the Free French War Relief, the USO, French prisoners, etc.

Some of the boys already have entered the United States armed forces or joined with de Gaulle, and they know that those who remain behind and enjoy the generous hospitality and traditional friendship of America will not stay idle.

We shall never see the same Paris or the same France we left. But none of us in Jeunesse France Libre want to see it the same. We want to see a better France, a better world—and we shall put the spirit of our youth to attain this goal.   BERNARD DARVILLE.

New York, Jan. 4, 1943.

Bernard signs his letter to the New York Times *with name Darville to avoid endangering his family in France. New York, 4 January 1943.* (Dargols Family Archive)

friends who had remained in the occupied zone were, one after the other, arriving in Monflanquin and relating the untenable situation and the increasing number of arrests. Sick at heart, Jean accepted the position in New York to protect his wife and two daughters.

In August 1941, Françoise left by train with her family for the city of Pau [50 miles from the Spanish border] then crossed into Spain and luckily managed to get on board the last ship, the *Exeter*, in Lisbon. They arrived and settled in New York

Françoise Dargols (right) on her graduation day at Columbia University. New York City, summer of 1947. (Dargols Family Archive)

in September 1941. There, her father founded the Free School
for Advanced Studies with several renowned professors such
as Professor Jacques Maritain and Claude Levi-Strauss. They
later learned that the Rockefeller Foundation had helped many
threatened public figures leave Europe during the war, as it had
done for Françoise's family, by paying for their visas and by
offering them jobs in the United States.

When I met Françoise, she was studying teacher education
at the Ann-Reno Institute in New York City. She later graduated
from Columbia University. She wanted to join our organization.
I asked her for twenty-five cents for the membership fee, and
that was our first encounter. Who would have known then that
she would become and still be my wife today? I like to remind
her that over seventy-one years, her twenty-five cents have
really paid off.

*Françoise Dargols (far right) in front of La Marseillaise association.
New York, 1942.* (Dargols Family Archive)

Françoise was also a volunteer with *La Marseillaise*, an organization located in a former shop turned canteen, at the corner of 2nd Avenue and 42nd East Street in New York. Sailors and soldiers of the *Forces Françaises Libres*, far from home, were welcomed there in an easy-going and family atmosphere while they waited for their ships to be resupplied with weapons and munitions and to set off again for England, to continue the war.

We were a good gang of friends at the time, and we often went out together. We were all broke, except one, who sometimes drove us out to Coney Island.

***

I lived on 544 W. 108th Street in Manhattan when the US Army's draft notice, which I was waiting for, finally landed in the mailbox almost a year after I volunteered.

Until 1941, the Americans were for a large part isolationist. They were at peace with Germany and Italy and refused to take part in a conflict which didn't concern them. They wouldn't consider sending their boys to fight in Europe, even if their sympathy was intuitively with their British 'cousins' and the France of La Fayette. They didn't feel threatened: why should they fear German attacks when the Nazis were unable of invading England. Obviously, everything changed on 7 December 1941 with Japan's surprise attack on the US naval base of Pearl Harbor. It was a Sunday. Japan had targeted the American military base in Hawaii, causing thousands of casualties to the Marines, and sinking many war ships. It was the beginning of war between the United States and Japan, and therefore against the Axis of Japan, Germany and Italy.

The attack on Pearl Harbor set the entire American industry in motion: the United States needed to create an army nearly from scratch, equipping itself with heavy and lightweight weapons, all types of ships, military vehicles, tanks, not to mention Jeeps to transport American troops thousands of kilometres away towards Japan. It was a major boost for the world's biggest industrial power, leading to Japan's defeat, and to the United States' becoming the Allied countries' arsenal.

Although Japan was their first enemy, its alliance with Nazi Germany drew the Americans into the war in Europe, and against Hitler. Before that, Americans saw no reason to send soldiers thousands of kilometres away to fight the Nazis, but this feeling changed. Hitler, Japan's ally, had also become the enemy to be defeated.

My draft orders were to go to Fort Dix, New Jersey, near New York City. I left the one-room apartment I had lived in for three years at the corner of Broadway and 113th Street. I had to part from Françoise. Although we weren't engaged, Françoise and I had decided to get married, if I came back from the war, preferably in one piece, and if our mutual feelings hadn't changed. I gave her a 5-franc-piece which my friend Maurice had cut in half and incorporated into a key-chain. She gave me a silver bracelet, my name engraved on it, which never left me.

One after the other my workshop friends were drafted. Almost all the New Yorkers went to Fort Dix, which was a training and transit camp where we traded civilian clothes for a uniform without knowing for how long. In a few days, I became a French man in a US soldier's uniform. I was getting acquainted with my new GI status 'Government Issued'.

CHAPTER 2

Basic Training

My joining the US Army put an end to months of bureaucratic procedures to obtain visas granting my father and brothers the right to set foot in America. Their ordeal had lasted eighteen months, including fourteen months stuck in Cuba where my brothers learned industrial diamond cutting, the only activity allowed to refugees in Cuba.

When they finally reached New York, they moved in with me in my studio. With some help from the boss of the factory where I was interning, my father opened a sewing machine store on 25th Street. Marcel, suffering from lung issues, couldn't enroll in the army but worked in an armament factory where he carved diamonds for the US air force, and would help out in the shop when he could. As for Simon, like me he enrolled in the US Army as soon as he was of age.

Upon arrival at the training camp I was handed a uniform by an officer who asked: 'And you, where are you from?' And whereas most others would say New York or Pennsylvania, I answered 'from Paris.' 'Paris, Texas?', 'No Paris, France.' He was amazed: 'Does that mean you wore a beret?' - 'Yes, often', 'And you did your shopping with a baguette tucked under your arm?' - 'Well of course.' 'And you ate croissants in the morning?' - 'Yes I did.' And further: 'And do you have the Légion d'Honneur?' As I told him I didn't he retorted 'ah, you see, then you aren't French!' Later my army mates were always friendly and keen to know more about France.

I was measured, weighed and given clothes and a pair of shoes. The latter was the subject of an elaborate ritual: each in turn, in our underwear, we stepped on a plate which looked like a scale, to which were added horizontal and vertical lines and many numbers and letters. On the plate, we were asked to lift two buckets of sand at arm's length, at which point our feet were at their widest. A soldier would then shout out the result, which for me was 9,5E. At the time in the US (as opposed to France) there were already two sizes per shoe, namely length and width. Today in France, seventy years later, I'm still offered a size 43 if a 42 is too narrow. I've never worn shoes more comfortable than those issued by the US Army in 1941.

At Fort Dix we were taught, among other things, to march in step, make U-turns when in line, handle a rifle. We also learned to salute properly, hands stretched out, fingers tightly held in alignment, forearm at a 45-degree angle. Then, we were meant to briskly bring the index to the eyebrow's right end, hold the position for a fraction of a second and finally bring the arm back against the body.

Wednesday, 27 January 1943: Fort Dix, NJ

Wake up at 5:30 am every day. Yesterday, IQ tests (I scored 129 out of 150 and 131-150). 110 is enough to enrol in the officers' school. Food is fairly good (terrible coffee) but Fort Dix is only short-term. No radio, naturally. Bought the Times *which tells me that Roosevelt and Churchill just wrapped up a conference on a war strategy for 1943, which lasted 10 days.*

Fort Dix was a short 2 or 3-week-stage to get into the swing of it and the beginning of a months long training in several camps. From Fort Dix I was sent to an immense military camp in South Carolina, Camp Croft, where, like all new GIs, I carried out my three months of Basic Training.

Camp Croft was huge, with large drill grounds and neatly aligned barracks. Discipline and schedules were very strict: we woke up very early and had to make our beds with hospital corners and without a single crease. I would put my stuff away in a trunk at the foot of my bed. Even if my blonde stubble seemed imperceptible the sergeant inspector made sure daily that we were well-shaved by brushing our cheeks with his hand, which forced us to stay impeccable.

The field manual, the soldier's little handbook, we were given upon our arrival became my bedside reading. It reminded us of the basics: how to salute, the proper way of wearing the uniform, the fundamentals of weapons, the badges and ranks, but also how to behave as GIs with civilians and how to be a good team member.

The day continued with endless hours of training. For instance, races and obstacles on various assault courses: we were to crawl flat on our stomachs as fast as possible for thirty yards or so, passing under barbed-wire 50 centimetres above ground and under bursts of real bullets fired from slightly overhead.

Camp Croft military camp, South Carolina, USA, 1943. The sign on the left for 'Ladies only' depicts the soldiers' humour in a male-only camp. (Dargols Family Archive)

Training for close combat with a bayonet and night walks became my daily routine. Armed with our bayonets we were required to run across a field and to plant the weapon in a succession of sand bags. When the weapon remained stuck in a bag, the sergeant would explain how to retrieve the bayonet by leaning on one's back leg and simultaneously shoving away the enemy's skewered body. For someone brought up to such gentle standards—'don't get into fights; be nice to your school mates; help elderly people; give up your seat in the bus'—what a contrast it was to receive these orders! What kind of fighting was I going to engage in?

We regularly went on 20-kilometre walks loaded with our soldier's kit. The sergeant would yell 'Chop, chop!' and 'On the double!' to goad us into increasing our pace.

During a manoeuvre in Tennessee I remember stopping by a peasant who was sharpening a stick as he leisurely see-sawed in the rocking chair on his porch. I asked him what he would do once the stick was done: he'd just start a new one.

Back at the camp we would line up, on our backs with our shoes and socks off. A medic would then

Françoise and Bernard. Central Park, New York City, 1943. Marcel Dargols is seen in the middle. (Dargols Family Archive)

inspect our feet. GIs' feet were always well cared for. We always ate on schedule and although I finally had the pleasure of eating my fill once in the army, I regularly had to put in the potato duty (KP or Kitchen Police), which wasn't all that fun.

At Camp Croft, I also touched my first weapon: the M1, a shotgun, which seemed terribly heavy to me. The instructing officer quickly introduced our rifle as being 'our best friend... Take good care of it, it may save your life!' My mother would doubtless have fainted if she'd seen me decked out like that. We had to learn how to take it apart and reassemble it blindfolded and as fast as possible. As a mechanic, it was very easy for me. It reminded me of my work on sewing machines, small mechanics in other words!

Thursday, 11 March 1943: Camp Croft, SC

This morning: long jump, rope climbing, track and field exercises followed by a fanning out drill in case of an air attack when on the road, and map reading. This afternoon: hike with the heavy pack for about 4 hours and two 10-minute-breaks. In the evening: went to see how to cross and cut the barbed wire. Received 2 cables from Papa.

Morale and health: excellent.

Sunday, 21 March 1943: Camp Croft, SC

On Saturday at 1.30 am, I was transferred from the 35th to the 29th battalion. I tremendously regretted leaving some officers and non-commissioned officers such as Lieutenants Parker, Walker and Sergeant Evans to whom I owe everything that I know of my military life.

All day long we assembled and dismantled the Browning machine gun. The company I belong to is in the Heavy Weapons section.

A 2-day leave allowed me to see Françoise back in New York. In my haste to go I left with my shotgun, disassembled and buried deep in my bag, which would have gotten me in big trouble had I been checked by an MP.

Upon our return, between 5 and 6 am, we lined up and the sergeant took a roll call to make sure no one had gone AWOL.[2] Whoever chanced it faced a disciplinary measure.

At Camp Croft we also had classes in real classrooms. After basic training, we were required to take written tests that were fairly easy and to answer several multiple-choice questionnaires of around forty questions. These were for example: naming New York state's capital, specifying the number of US senators or drawing the major rivers of France on a blank map. Clearly, as the three months of basic training reached their term, these tests and the interviews with officers were designed to assign us to one or another section of the army: the infantry, artillery, medical corps, tankers or engineers. We were incorporated into the section where we would best serve the army. Given my good physical shape I took for granted I was destined for the infantry. I expected to be enrolled as a foot soldier for an infantry camp, the artillery or tanks, and maybe, owing to my mechanics skills, to be tasked with the maintenance of the rolling equipment, from jeeps to tanks. I also had more than enough mathematical knowledge to be incorporated into the artillery. Driving a tank or a jeep, repairing vehicles were also right up my street.

One day in mid-1943 I received my assignment to Camp Ritchie, Maryland, near Washington, DC, to join the Military Intelligence Service. No one around me had ever heard about Camp Ritchie; all my mates were sent to other training camps. And so it was that I left them behind and went towards the unknown.

A few weeks before joining Camp Ritchie, I was summoned by a senior officer. He laid out the situation:

If you end up fighting in France as a French man embedded with the US Army and wearing the US uniform, and you are made prisoner in your country of origin, you will be considered a spy by the enemy. You'll be on your own. However, if you'd like to, you could become a US citizen without losing your French citizenship, in which case you'd be treated like any other American soldier.

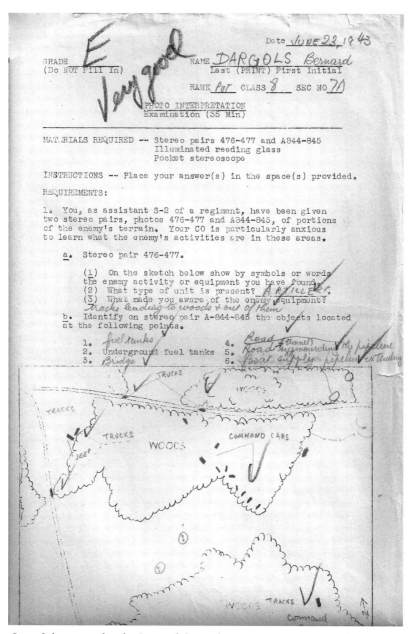

One of the tests taken by Bernard during his training at Camp Ritchie.
(Dargols Family Archive)

Bernard and his father, Paul. South Carolina, USA, April 1943. (Dargols Family Archive)

I accepted the offer and travelled to Spartenburg, North Carolina, where it took only a few minutes for a law court to grant me US citizenship.

- 'Raise your hand and say *I do*.'
- 'I do.'

The army offered to change my name. I could have chosen Bernard Roosevelt or Bernard Sinatra for a laugh, but I preferred to keep my father's name, Dargols.

Saturday, 3 April 1943: Camp Croft, SC

Today I became a US citizen.

APRIL 3   1943

Camp Croft, N.C.   Samedi -

Je suis devenu citoyen

américain, aujourd'hui -

Extract from Bernard's diary dated 3 April 1943. 'Today I became an American citizen.' (Dargols Family Archive)

CHAPTER 3

Camp Ritchie: Military Intelligence Service

'The main thing to beat the enemy isn't strength but ruse: one needs to trick the enemy, unsettle him, disorganize him with an unexpected approach, as a result creating a weak point and making use of it to the greatest extent.'[6]

Jean Deuve

After Camp Croft, Camp Ritchie felt like a small college campus. Inside the camp there were large buildings with rooms that looked like classrooms and amphitheatres. It was the only secret Military Intelligence camp in the US and I was about to learn the techniques specific to this section of the army. But I never understood why, if it was meant to be secret, the name 'Military Intelligence T.C.' figured distinctly at the camp's entrance. The people of the nearby small town Hagerstown knew nothing of the meaning of the letters T.C., which in fact only stood for Training Center.

The Camp was divided into several sections. The first and most imposing, the IPW Section (Interrogation of Prisoners of War), included soldiers who learned how to interrogate German prisoners of war. The second one, Section PI (Photo Interpreter), studied documents which the reconnaissance planes brought back after flying over enemy facilities or fortifications. This for example allowed the PI to spot the blockhouses built by the Germans along the coast. It also provided relief views of the

Some of Bernard's friends at Camp Ritchie, Maryland, 1943. (Dargols Family Archive)

Normandy coastline of 1944, with its village churches, fields and farms. All this was incredibly new to me. I belonged to the third section MII (for Military Intelligence Interpreter), otherwise known as the French section, whose mission was to interrogate French civilians in the event of a landing in France. The term 'intelligence' referred to its etymology, that is, to 'understand' and, likewise, the 'interpreter' wasn't the person translating but knowledgeably analysing information.

Our teachers—some were officers, others business managers—taught us how to lead psychological warfare: I learned to spot strategic locations and gather information and how to ask civilians the crucial questions. The goal was to gain as much intelligence in a given time and to figure it out as fast as possible to identify the enemy we were going to face. Speaking and writing French was mandatory and explained why I hadn't been assigned elsewhere in the army, unlike the thousands of trainees from my division.[7] French collaborationists such as

Darlan, Doriot[8] and the *Pilori*, *Gringoire* or *Je suis Partout* newspapers held no secrets for me. In the event of a landing in France, my knowledge of the country, of its geography, history and language were major assets to question civilians without mistakes or misunderstandings. My primary mission was neither to kill nor to learn how to kill but above all to gather tactical or even strategic intelligence on the enemy, thus allowing our units to make headway. I wasn't especially keen on carrying a weapon: it went totally against the grain of the education I had been given. But it was indispensable to defend myself.

The nature of our training at Camp Ritchie had to remain strictly secret. We were sworn to secrecy, even from our wives. I was instructed to say I was an interpreter at an infantry camp. I wasn't allowed to give any kind of information to my family: neither where I was nor what I really did. To avoid leaks on our whereabouts the address of Camp Ritchie didn't even figure on our mail.

In fact I've only allowed myself to use its name since 2005 after a TV broadcast of the documentary titled *The Ritchie Boys*.[5] The film depicted the camp's section devoted to the training of American soldiers who spoke German and would interrogate the prisoners of war (IPW Section).

Shooting practice, manoeuvres and route marches continued day and night. A frequent exercise occurred at night in the hills of Maryland, the Blue Ridge Mountains. Around 10 or 11 pm we were packed into trucks and let loose one by one on a road approximately every 300 meters. The goal was to regroup at midnight at a given place and to return together to the camp. I played the part of the French civilian, wearing a black armband to be recognized as such. My group comrades were to question me concerning an enemy potentially present in the vicinity. For the most part they were well educated and did their utmost to speak good French but it was incredibly easy for me to exasperate them. We slept in tents and sometimes in the dead of the night we had to pack up and go at full speed, either to chase the enemy or because the enemy was chasing us. During the manoeuvres, we were forbidden from entering any house whatsoever—inhabited or not—under penalty of a

$75 fine. Often, during our rushed moves, we ran out of time to eat, especially considering that the kitchen truck was the first to leave. Luckily my small team was very resourceful and managed to store food which some farmers sold us on the sly. We rode jeeps throughout the night without sleeping. We practised interrogating prisoners impersonated by other soldiers. I also learned Morse code in a record eight weeks time but I never was in a position to use it and forgot it just as quickly.

During our infrequent 24-hour leaves all the soldiers went to Hagerstown, the village located just a few kilometers away from the camp. There was just enough time to go to the restaurant, gobble up a wonderful T-bone steak and return to the camp.

A French/English dictionary of military terms now replaced my field manual. I had to commit to memory pages and pages of detailed information on the make-up and weapons of the units from every country involved in the war. During these long hours of class I memorized the exact composition of an SS Panzer division[6]: the number of men, their ranks, vehicles, the amount

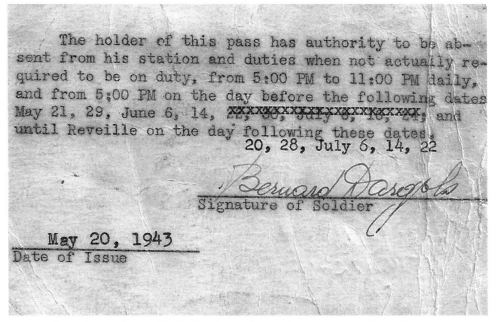

Pass given to Bernard in 1943 allowing him to leave the camp. (Dargols Family Archive)

of canons, their calibres and range. Likewise, with the other German Army divisions, and their British, French or Italian counterparts. Later, in Normandy, when a civilian described the shape of a German soldier's badge I knew right away which unit he belonged to and how many men it comprised. I could then report the information to my division.

After a few weeks, I was promoted: I had to question the Camp's newcomers and give them a grade. I asked them to read a page from Chateaubriand in order to determine their level of French, which I'd easily verify by asking them to translate the expression 'remarques dénigrantes'. Those who correctly answered 'disparaging remarks' were very proficient. One day Maurice Shire, the friend from New York with whom I'd created the Jeunesse France Libre, showed up. It was a ludicrous situation: I knew full well he spoke excellent French and the test quickly turned into a joyful reunion. In the following days, whenever I passed by his classroom I would tease him by whistling 'Oh, What a beautiful morning, Oh, What a beautiful day.'[7]

It was also in the MII at Camp Ritchie that I met Eddie Coleman, a brilliant man gifted with an outstanding memory. Eddie was from California. He enjoyed tap dancing and we shared the same sense of humour and taste for jazz. We stayed friends long after the war.

Although light heartedness was de rigueur among the trainees, we began to feel restless: how much longer would our training last? Where would we go once it was over? Maybe in the Pacific region? I dreaded that option. At least if we landed in Europe I could hope to get closer to my family.

After nine months of training at Camp Ritchie our civilian interrogation team was finally formed, composed of six men who spoke good or even excellent French, thus answering the following question: what was the point of speaking French if it was to wind up in the Pacific? I understood that in any event we would land in Europe, if not in France. It was a huge relief for me despite the fact that the departure date remained the big unknown.

**

We left Camp Ritchie on 15 December 1943, and headed for a new training camp in Wales, United Kingdom, where we spent almost six months to the day. Before leaving, everyday we would read in the newspapers that convoys bound for England were again and again sunk by German U-boats. The Queen Elizabeth was to take us to England by way of Scotland without any escort. We were warned that our high-speed ship—loaded with specialists— would zig-zag its way to England thus preventing German submarines from adjusting their shots. As a result, she wouldn't be escorted by warships. The prospect was rather frightening.

We thus boarded the SS *Queen Elizabeth*. Soldiers aboard had a passion for gambling, especially card games, which kept our minds off things. To avoid detection by enemy ships, smoking above deck was forbidden after dusk. The Atlantic Ocean was swarming with U-boats attacking Allied ships,[8] in particular the numerous convoys transporting weapons, ammunition and spare parts towards Britain. Escorted for a few miles convoys advanced slowly, at the same pace as their slowest ship. The *Queen Elizabeth* took thousands of us across the ocean without mishap, and we arrived safe and sound in Scotland. From there we were dispatched towards various locations unknown to us. I was part of the group taken by train to Wales, more precisely to Tenby harbour,

Bernard Dargols in his office in Tenby, Wales, 1944. (Dargols Family Archive)

in Pembrokeshire. An office was waiting for me in the village, which resembled the ports of Brittany and felt a little closer to home. For a very short time I joined the 28th Infantry Division.

I was promptly separated from my five teammates and sent to a secluded camp in Eastern Wales, at St Donat's Castle, a medieval castle approximately 30 kilometers from Cardiff. This very secret location was so well hidden that I was afraid I would never find my way back when returning from leave. In Wales training took a very different turn. My team and I were assigned to the US 2nd Infantry Division. My rifle was replaced with a sub-machine gun and a handgun: this indicated that I would probably be a close-range combatant.

While combat training continued, I was entrusted with a 'psychological' task: I needed to prepare the GIs for the landing by describing, in English of course, what they should expect to find in France. That is how on several occasions I found myself facing a hundred GIs sitting on a grassy slope, an open-air amphitheatre of sorts. They listened for about an hour and asked me a multitude of questions about France and French habits. At first I really had stage-fright, but after a few minutes and some joking around, it would disappear and I'd feel much more comfortable.

What mattered to them most was when and where we would take on the enemy. I was instructed to say that we would most likely land in the Northern France, in the city of Calais. None of us knew the exact location of our future landing. Calais seemed obvious coming from England: the crossing would be short. I couldn't answer them concerning the 'when', not having been told either. They all wanted to get it over with as soon as possible and go home. It was different for me. I was drawing closer to France and my family in Paris and hoping to finally be reunited with them after six years of absence.

The GIs asked if milk in France was pasteurized. At the time, American adults drank lots of milk while only young children drank milk in France. They wondered if they would be welcomed by the French people. I explained that if we landed in France it wouldn't be to invade a hostile country but to liberate a friendly one from the Nazi occupier. 'Not to invade but to land in France.' I also insisted on the importance of following orders not to buy food from the farmers or locals: I described the situation in France, the country's complex troubles, the STO,[9] the food rationing, the result of which was the French people's daily and greatest preoccupation with finding food. Naturally they also wanted to know if French girls were as pretty as they were claimed to be. They were surprized to learn that Texas was bigger than mainland France. When to wrap up the talk I told them that Paris was 300 kilometers or 190 miles from Calais, they instantly envisioned themselves at the Eiffel Tower!

I answered as best I could but sorely missed my geography books. During these field lectures, we also learned how to differentiate tanks and planes not just by their shapes but above all thanks to the sounds they produced. Amplifiers would broadcast recorded sounds, teaching us to tell the difference between approaching German, English and American tanks, or between an English Spitfire and a German Stuka plane.[10]

Still, we had no clue concerning the date or exact location of the landing.

The preparation for the upcoming landing was thorough and intense. These manoeuvres and training carried on for six months. Night exercises kept us on our toes. Like the Camp Croft routine, we were let out of a truck one by one in the dead of the night, with a map of the area and a compass, and ordered to regroup in a given spot at midnight sharp. I have no sense of direction and was invariably amazed not to miss the truck taking us back.

Over and over we practised riding down a ramp in the sand without getting our jeep stuck.

Route marches ended at the camp. Once the medic had inspected our swollen feet we would make our way to the movie theatre with its perfect sound system and seats so comfortable that few of us managed to stay awake through a whole movie, not even Frank Capra's *Why We Fight*. In February 1942 Capra was assigned to the Signal Corps' cinematography department and seconded to the Morale Branch. General Marshall called

V-mail from Bernard sent from Wales to his brother, Simon, who was stationed in Florida, USA, in 1944. (Dargols Family Archive)

upon him to '... tell our young men why they must become soldiers and why they need to fight. These films are an absolute necessity.' Capra became a producer for the army and directed

Why We Fight. The goal was to unite Americans in the war effort and to explain why enlisting in the army was so crucial. I remember I enjoyed these screenings as brief interludes in our daily training. Following these screenings were those reserved to the black units: sadly, the US Army was an accurate reflection of the country's segregation at the time.

During that same stretch of time in Britain I came to learn why the Russian port of Murmansk was shrouded in secrecy. An English sailor who couldn't hold his tongue let slip that American convoys unloaded in the Soviet port their shipments of weapons and spare parts—especially engines destined to Soviet tanks. The Americans tried to avoid leaks in order to foil potential bombings of these convoys or attacks by enemy submarines. As for the Russians, they kept quiet about the major help the US was providing them and their ensuing reliance on another country, which ran against their political pride.

***

Over five months went by in this remote camp at St Donat's Castle in Wales. Time seemed endless. We were eager to land, fight, drive out the German Army and above all, go home. All the GIs wanted to get the job done, well done for sure, but also quickly.

In April and May 1944, we started to notice gradual changes to our daily routine which all pointed to our departure and destination. Firstly, food which had always been abundant but plain seemed to improve by the day. We would never run out of cigarettes - I smoked Chesterfields. We were also provided with C rations, a kind of canned stew.

Our individual weapons, handguns and sub-machine guns, maps, compasses, food rations and rations were increasingly inspected. We were no longer allowed to write or receive any mail whatsoever. At that point, I warned my father not worry about my silence as my letters were bound to be few and far between.

Bernard and Toto McCormick, April/May 1944. (Dargols Family Archive)

HQ, 28th Inf. Div

APO28, c/o P'master N.Y, N.Y

Britain, 12 April 1944

Dear Papa,

I am writing to you from the US Red Cross. As usual, everything is going well. The radio here is swell. I easily tuned into Radio Paris and listened to the news. It started with Giraud and De Gaulle arguing and ended with the advance of the Red Army towards Odessa. I didn't believe that, as ten minutes before the French radio in London had announced the capture of the port! The Allies have taken Odessa; I suppose you celebrated with the best whiskey you had. And you'd be amazed to learn what's going on in France these days. I am very optimistic. Don't forget that if you receive less letters from me, it is because I am going to be very busy, so please don't worry.

Bernard.

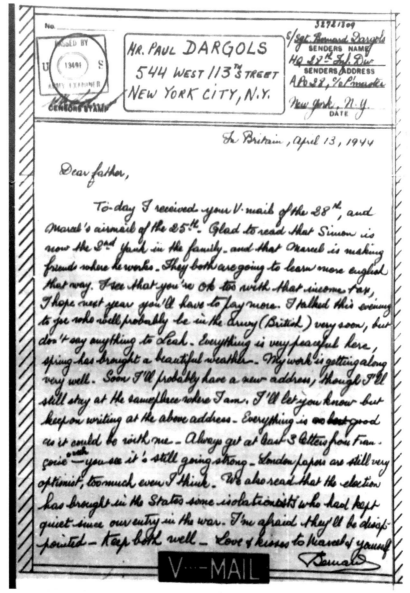

V-mail sent from Bernard while in Britain to his father in New York. April, 1944.
(Dargols Family Archive)

We were granted many 24-hour leaves, of which I took advantage to visit my aunts, uncles and cousins in London. My mother's two sisters hadn't emigrated to France with their parents and my mother. Miriam ran a candy shop in London and lived in Hackney, a close suburb. Leah lived in Wanstead, a well-to-do neighbourhood of London. Wartime London was teeming with soldiers from all nations and I saw women from the WAC for the first time. I was also introduced to the V1 and V2, the German flying bombs with their unmistakable whistling. The sound of a motorbike engine that stops short. The airborne bombs continue on their way, silently, for ten more seconds before crashing on the city. The moment of silence before the explosion was very upsetting; Londoners knew they needed to take shelter right away. The V1 and V2 caused terrible damage.

I told my father about one of them:

> *I was at the Belsons during the biggest air raid since the Americans have been in Britain. The DCA[10] did a good job. Shrapnel fell in the garden. Betty and Miriam were quite scared. The house's windowpanes were shaking and for a moment we thought there were incendiary bombs in the garden. I went to see outside.*

> *The sound of German engines, the exploding shells: Believe me, it was really impressive!*

> *I quite unexpectedly ran into Maurice Shire and another friend from the* Jeunesse France Libre *right here in London. What a coincidence that was!'*

On 4 April 1944, I wrote to my brother who had enrolled in the US Army:

> *Dear Simon,*

> *I see that your training is carrying on quite similar to mine. During the 13 weeks of training, if yours last as long as mine, you can expect several hikes with full-field-pack,*

for long as well as short hikes. I found that two pairs of woollen socks made them more acceptable. However, the socks must fit well [in English in the letter]. *Especially not too long!*

First you will follow a fair amount of bayonet training. I, too, was with the Heavy weapons unit. At about the middle of your basic [training], you will get acquainted with the 30-calibre machine gun, water cooled, and with the mortar.

These are the 2 weapons called heavy. It's much better to be with this unit than with the regular rifle platoon. It's much more interesting. The weapons are heavy to carry and drag. You'll shoot with both, you'll also crawl under sub-machine guns firing above your head. But that's nothing. To me basic training is much harder. Some very useful stuff is in your book, the field manual. You'll get promoted faster if you know what's in there. 'You'll be on the ball!' [in English in the text] *But I'm*

Simon Dargols during his US Army training at Camp Blanding. Florida, USA, April 1944. (Dargols Family Archive)

*warning you it's really tough to move up to a higher rank
in infantry! Congrats Yankee!*

Everything is going very well.

Kisses

Bernard

Back at the camp, rumours of our departure were growing. We
tried to ignore them. In April 1944 Eisenhower came in person
to deliver a speech, which we considered another sign that our
training was coming to an end. Day in and day out we'd hear
'tomorrow we're embarking'. The wait was nerve-racking, much
like the growing fear of a patient whose operation is unexpectedly
but repeatedly put off to the following day. I was asked to make
a will and choose its recipient. What an odd feeling it was to
draft a will in favour of my father at the age of twenty.

That's when I realized our departure was about to happen.
It felt liberating.

The landing's location remained secret. The camp was
alive with rumours: one rumour held that we were going to
land in Norway, occupied by the Germans... why Norway? The
Americans had discreetly asked neutral Sweden for the right to
fly over the country. Another rumour predicted the Southern
coast of Brittany; the most persistent rumours pointed at Calais
or Boulogne. Hadn't I, myself, been instructed to say that the
landing would probably take place in France in the area of
Calais? In any event, all these rumours proclaimed that 'It's
happening tomorrow!' It was always happening tomorrow.

It seemed increasingly obvious that the operation would
occur somewhere between Belgium and Southern Brittany.
All along that coastline the Allied air-force, a few days before
the landing, had dropped thousands of double-sided 'Urgent
Message' fliers urging the population to move inland due to the
bombings that would happen before long.

All these calculated or candid rumours, to which I had in
fact contributed, were designed to force the enemy to regroup in
the region of Calais. This was *Operation Fortitude*.

LAST WILL AND TESTAMENT

I, __Bernard Dargols__, now serving in the Army of the United States, with legal residence at __544 W. 113th St., N.Y., N.Y.__, do hereby make, publish and declare this to be my Last Will and Testament, hereby expressly revoking any and all other Will or Wills heretofore executed by me.

ITEM ONE - I direct that all my just debts, funeral expenses and the cost of administration upon my estate shall be paid out of my estate.

ITEM TWO - All the rest, residue and remainder of my estate, real, personal, or mixed, wherever situate and however acquired, including any property over which I may have power of testamentary disposition, I give, devise and bequeath unto __my father Paul Dargols, same address__ and __his__ heirs and assigns forever.

ITEM THREE I nominate and appoint __my father Paul Dargols, same address__ to be the Execut(or)(_____) of this my Last Will and Testament, and desire that the usual fiduciary bond for faithful performance not be required.

IN WITNESS WHEREOF, I have hereunto set my hand and seal this __30__ day of __Nov.__, 1943.

Bernard Dargols SEAL

SIGNED, SEALED, PUBLISHED AND DECLARED, by __Bernard Dargols__, the above named Testator, as and for his Last Will and Testament, in the presence of us and each of us, who, at his request and in his presence, and in the presence of each other have hereunto subscribed our names as subscribing and attesting witnesses, this __30__ day of __Nov.__, 1943.

Paul W. Stely __33232560__ Camp Ritchie, Maryland.

John H. Masick __33245966__ Camp Ritchie, Maryland

Donald R. Lothrop __33230913__ Camp Ritchie, Maryland

The will Bernard had to sign in 1943 before leaving for Normandy. (Dargols Family Archive)

In the dark of the night dozens of inflatable rubber tanks, jeeps and trucks were deployed near Dover. They were meant to be detected by German surveillance and have them believe in a concentration of Allied forces in preparation of a landing in Calais. I remember that even close up these dummies bore an eerie resemblance to their real counterparts. A finishing touch consisted in dozens of airborne paratroopers, inflatable dolls in actual fact. This subterfuge of huge military means, a veritable ghost army stationed in Dover, lent total credibility to the rumours we'd initiated. The Operation was a real success: disinformation and propaganda led everybody astray. Hitler himself believed the landing would happen in Calais and subsequently the German forces were rounded up in the region. The German general-staff, however, leaned towards a landing in Normandy. Major General Leonard T. Gerow, who among others later masterminded Operation Overlord but also a plan involving a 'fake' Paris during World War I, staged a similar operation in June 1943: Operation Wadham, ostensibly a plan to land in Brittany, was a total hoax orchestrated by the army.

A few days before the landing, I wrote to my father:

England, 22 May 1944

Papa,

Did I tell you that when I left my little place on the coast, my team and I gathered for a feast in our office with caviar, gin and lemon?

Don't worry if my address changes again, it doesn't mean anything, I'm telling you again, I have every reason to be happy but I can't tell you why.

Bernard

CHAPTER 4

The Landing

[…] And Crispin Crispian shall ne'er go by,

From this day to the ending of the world

But we in it shall be remembered

We few, we happy few, we band of brothers;

For he today that sheds his blood with me

Shall be my brother […]

King Henry V, William Shakespeare

The moment of departure arrived on 4 June 1944. We were ordered to pack up and go. Our kit was ready. So we left the camp that night for an unknown destination, which we had a feeling was going to be extremely difficult. We were in excellent physical and psychological shape and happy to finally get started. A steam train was waiting to take us from Pembroke to Cardiff, to our great surprise: we thought that to reach Calais it would make more sense to leave from Dover or Folkestone.

On 5 June we embarked aboard a Liberty ship, a troopship about 110 meters long, of the kind the US had been churning out by the thousands for two years.

I sat on board with my five comrades and dozens of other GIs, pressed together on benches. My team had been formed a few weeks earlier and comprised six men: two officers, Lieutenant Wrenn, a journalist at the *New Yorker*, and Lieutenant

Menzel; Technical Sergeant Thierry McCormick, known as Toto and the member with whom I had the most in common; Corporal Gladstone and Sergeant Hans Namuth who was a famous photographer. Hans, Toto and I became friends and we got along very well. Just like I was interrogated at Ritchie, I later had to interrogate Hans to whom I gave a favourable recommendation. His story seemed truly incredible. Hans, who was older than me, was born in Germany and had been forced to enrol in the Hitler Youth by his father, a notorious Nazi. But bad blood and contrariness had driven him away from home and

On the Liberty Ship. The English Channel, 5 June 1944. (Dargols Family Archive)

he joined the Spanish anti-Fascists in 1936. He was the only member of the team with a genuine military experience. I am indebted to him for most of the photographs of our journey. As for me, I had been promoted directly to staff sergeant without going through the intermediate ranks. We were provided with a complete equipment: two jeeps and a trailer, camouflage nets, and gas masks—which I never used. As members of the Military Intelligence Service, each of us was given a kind of nail to be pushed into walls to hear what was happening on the other side, which turned out to be rather useless, as well as a Hamilton chronometer wristwatch—at the time a very precious object.

Bad weather delayed our departure. The Liberty ship's captain opened an envelope enclosing the mission order with the itinerary to follow: we were going to France. Aboard the Liberty ship, soldiers crammed against each other in the hold, the atmosphere quickly became stuffy. Even then we had no idea where the landing would occur, or if it would actually happen. In fact, D-Day was drawing closer. Apprehension took hold of us all. I remembered President Franklin D. Roosevelt's words, 'We have nothing to fear but fear itself'.[11]

No one was talking. The sea swell was strong and the waves rhythmically collided against the hull of the boat. Hours went by and our ship hadn't moved away from the English coast. We were aware that the training was over and that the serious stuff had started.

On 6 June we were still trapped in the increasingly confined atmosphere of the hold when finally, our Liberty ship raised anchor and left on her own. As we began our slow progress across the Channel, powerful waves began rocking the boat. A choppy sea made the crossing very difficult. For many hours, we were at a standstill, tossing about in the heavy seas, then pitching and rolling as the ship slowly moved forward. Heat, fatigue, fear of the unknown, all seemed to conspire against us. Owing to the adventure ahead, we just couldn't joke around any more. I realized how lucky I was not to be prone to seasickness, which afflicted many of my comrades. Moreover, in this sea swarming with U-boats, we feared that at any moment our boat would be targeted. We were terrified by the airborne attacks that had destroyed many of our ships and could just as well bring a brutal end to our seemingly endless trip.

We rotated on eight hour shifts: while some stayed above deck, others rested in the bunk beds down in the hold. We were making a very long detour to reach the French coast. Where would we land? I wondered how many hours would pass, how many days separated us from our destination? Knowing neither the journey's itinerary, length or end, we were overwhelmed with doubt and apprehension. Could we make it through the crossing unharmed? It was our only obsession at that point.

On the boat, I observed my fellow soldiers with their helmets and weapons, relatively confident and eager to land so as to get it over with and return home as fast as possible. I wondered if, in due course, they would remember my field lectures. The goal was not to invade France but to liberate it from the Nazi occupiers. After all, France was a friend and ally.

We thought we would be the first soldiers to set foot on the beach. I was hoping we would take the enemy by surprise, not out of bravery but for a better chance to pull through. But as we steered around Wales and headed south and east of England, our boat was joined by one, then ten, then a hundred and even thousands of vessels: other Liberty ships, but also small crafts as well as immense and imposing warships.[12] Monstrous-looking blimps flew over most of the boats, tethered to them by means of metal ropes designed to deter enemy planes from drawing too close, at risk of getting entangled. These 'barrage balloons', which we dubbed 'sausages', somehow looked frightening. It was an incredible sight and hard to imagine. I was in awe of the extent of the operation. How could such large numbers not be detected by the enemy. I feared that the Germans, hidden in the blockhouses which lent them perfectly unobstructed views of the horizon, would scrutinize the sea and retaliate in a substantial way. Nevertheless, I had the strange feeling that if by chance I managed to set foot on French soil, I would somehow pull through.

We feared the German planes and warships which, however, were almost non-existent; only a few Allied planes could be seen. I later learned that Hitler, even a month after 6 June 1944, remained convinced that the armada headed for the beaches of Normandy was merely a diversion. He sent no backup troops, and kept in reserve his troops where they were, clinging to the notion that the real landing would occur in the Pas-de-Calais. Come to think about it, maybe Hitler saved my life!

For three days, the Liberty ship circled around the same spot before finally crossing the Channel. On 8 June we caught sight of the coast. I saw that it was France without recognising the exact location. We remained clueless about where we would set foot on the beach. During these three days, we had expected the attack to be airborne rather than submarine, but we'd seen very few German planes flying overhead and no enemy submarines.

Little by little the landscape came into focus as the Liberty ship approached Vierville-sur-Mer, as I later learned it was called. This was on the section of the coast bearing the codename Omaha Beach, stretching from Bayeux to Carentan.

Approximately 100 meters from the beach, an LCVP (Landing Craft Vehicle & Personnel) came alongside us. We got off the starboard side of the Liberty ship, scaling down a very unstable rope ladder onto the landing craft where my jeep, *La Bastille*, was waiting for us. We had been trained for many things but unfortunately not to climb down moving ropes, loaded with our kit, a sub-machine gun on our backs, between two boats that were also moving! That is one of my worst memories. I thought I'd never make it. The ladder refused to stay still long enough to touch the barge. Emotion overcame my concentration. The unbelievable noise of our bombing and shooting towards the coast invaded my brain: here and now a bomb could very well wipe us out. GIs were collapsing in the water, so how on earth was I supposed to make it across these last few meters? On the Liberty ship, all of us were scared but being surrounded by my comrades was truly heartening. At that moment between two boats the thought crossed my mind that if the Liberty ship had a back-pedal like my jeep, I'd have wanted someone to press down on it. When I finally reached the landing craft, my dread increased tenfold. I felt very alone. The darkness was constantly lit up by explosions and bombardments and you couldn't even tell where they were coming from. To these noises were added the whistling of shells and we had the impression that the war for us might finish right here in the water, before we even reached the beach. I thought how stupid it would be to die within 100 meters of France.

My recent training suddenly seemed very distant. I became aware that this was the 'real thing' and that I was embarking on a precarious journey. More than ever, I needed to be strong.

GIs burdened with their heavy kit continued to climb down the Liberty ship one by one and join us in the hold of the LCVP. There, dozens of military vehicles, trucks, jeeps, tanks, were poised to land on 'Easy Red', the Omaha Beach sector located between Saint-Laurent-sur-Mer and Vierville. The landing craft advanced quickly then stopped. Slowly it drew closer to the shore. The whole process seemed to have taken ages. We waited for new orders. Another half an hour passed before the huge ramp at the front of the craft began unfolding. Thirty minutes that seemed endless to us, stuck in a windowless hold flooded with the unrelenting noise of bombings. I was overwhelmed by the idea of returning to France and above all to my family. Six years earlier I had left France as a teenager. On the afternoon of 8 June 1944, I was returning as a GI. I was twenty-four years old.

The signal was sounded. Toto, Wrenn and I took ours seats in *La Bastille*, while our other three comrades got in the other jeep. We wished each other good luck. Each wave of assault was preceded by bombings so intense that we could feel them deep within our guts. I will never forget how I was taken over by fear and the deafening noise. A feeling of chaos. Shells fired from American ships flew over our heads. The aim: to secure the GIs' arrival on the beach. The loud noise of the warships' guns pounding the sector in front of us, mixed in with anti-aircraft fire, became deafening. In the midst of this confusion and agitation, the activity of the German Luftwaffe had seemed to me to be slight in comparison with that of the Allies'.

Jeeps in front of us started their engines. Toto was driving ours; he was the best driver. As we had learned during training, we went down the ramp onto the beach at top speed to avoid getting bogged down. It was low tide and once off the landing craft we rode a few dozen yards through some water before reaching the sand line. Some kind of putty had been applied around the jeep's lights to make them watertight. I had the feeling that each and every detail had been considered in order to make the landing successful.

In the water, I caught sight of the inert bodies of GIs, which the medics, identifiable thanks to their armbands and the red crosses on their helmets, hastened to bring to the shore. The carcasses of boats and tanks revealed the violence of the unfolding events. War correspondent Ernest Pyle described the scene in these words:

Men sleep on the sand next to other men asleep forever. Others float in the sea, but don't know they're in the water: they are dead. I walk along this long stretch of coast, witness to our landing, for a mile and a half. I walk slowly because countless details catch the eye on this beach. It's appalling to see such amounts of wreckage. On the dry beach itself, there are all manners of vehicles turned into scrap. There are tanks shredded to pieces just as they reached the beach. There are jeeps burnt to ashes, of a dull grey colour. There are huge cranes on caterpillar tracks, stranded close to the end. There are tracked vehicles loaded with office supplies, reduced to shrapnel by a single bombshell; they still show whole collections, now useless, of pulverized typewriters, telephones, ring binders. There are heavy barges, completely upturned, hull overhead; I can't understand what has happened to them? There are boats piled on top of each other, their hulls collapsed, doors torn off. In this museum of destruction on a pebble beach, there are rolls of barbed-wire, smashed excavators, heaps of lifebelts and piles of bombshells still waiting to be transported. On this beach are, lost forever, enough men and equipment to wage a small war.[13]

Once I set foot on the beach, a tremendous emotion choked me up.

The activity there was unbelievable: Omaha Beach was bustling with soldiers. Dozens of jeeps and trucks carrying fuel and supplies were piled up on either side of a sand path cleared of mines. The 300 meters of path led to the large sand dunes and hills of Saint-Laurent-sur-Mer, through a surreal landscape strewn with hundreds of obstacles: planted at a slant were enormous pieces of rails, a meter and a half high, resembling jaws ready to tear our ships to shreds. Higher up on the beach we passed by a casemate known as the Ruquet, whose 55 mm gun had already been neutralized by the GIs that came before us. Lines of infantry GIs, one behind the other, scaled a farm road leading to the front-line. How was I to know that, some sixty-five years later, this road would bear my name? In our jeep, Thierry McCormick and I followed it in the direction of the General Headquarters, some 5 or 6 kilometers away in

Formigny, where we had been ordered to go as fast as possible. Our teammates followed in the other jeep, but we would be sent to different places. From this steep road, I could make out ditches dug by the enemy and covered with branches, traps set up for our tanks to fall into. Meanwhile, the bombing of our ships continued with its terrible din.

At the same time, treading that same farm road—now paved—the medics carried down dozens of wounded or dead soldiers to have them evacuated by boat towards England. I was well aware of how lucky I was to be alive and still able to fight. Like me, most of my fellow GIs, also in their twenties, were seeing dead people for the first time. The word 'war' was now embodied by an implacable reality, where the impossible must be done to pull through alive. I admired my brothers-in-arms all the more so because they were fighting to liberate a country they didn't know, thousands of miles from home. Unlike me, they had no specific reason to fight against the Nazi occupier. Since Pearl Harbor, the Americans' enemy was really Japan more than Germany.

The mission of Operation Overlord launched by the Allies was to unload dozens of thousands of men on the coast of Normandy. We knew next to nothing about the previous landing and the 3,000 men who had lost their lives there, two days prior. I later learned that the Americans had renamed the beach 'Bloody Omaha', because Omaha Beach was where they had suffered the largest loss of human lives during the Second World War. The dunes lining the beaches were ideal hideouts for the Germans. This helped the 352nd Panzer Division, which had reached the area a few days earlier, fend off the arrival of the first American units on the beach. The Allied bombings were made difficult by poor visibility brought on by bad weather and they hadn't been able to neutralize the blockhouses by the beaches or the Atlantic Wall. The latter, a discontinuous line of obstacles, was unfinished, but nevertheless reinforced the German resistance, thereby contributing to the bloodshed of Allied soldiers.

In spite of these nightmarish scenes, I remained optimistic. All had been worked out and foreseen with means colossal enough to reach our goals. I was convinced we were going to win the war.

At the top of the road overlooking Omaha Beach we reached the Plateau du Ruquet, 50 meters or so above the coastline. In the distance, we could make out the outlines of the cliffs of Utah and Gold. The road ran along some vast grounds which were quickly turned into an air-runway. From 9 June our dead or wounded soldiers were evacuated to England by plane rather than by boat. A dreadful smell emanated from the surrounding fields, from dead animals and bloated cows; it was a smell I will never forget. It was actually the first time I had seen cows.

The visibility from the extremely narrow tree-lined road—a tunnel of greenery—was poor: a delight for snipers. On the road to the little village of Formigny, where the Germans had retreated, we came under fire from some of these isolated snipers. Whistling bullets came out of nowhere and had us ducking down again and again, but none of this prevented our progress. The division captured its first prisoners, which I eyed with some satisfaction. The road from Isigny to Bayeux really had to be taken from the Germans.

McCormick and I were impatient to reach the General HQ: at last our real mission would begin.

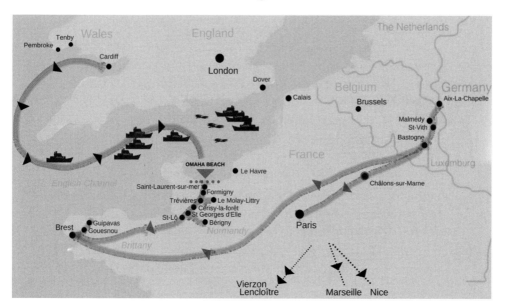

CHAPTER 5

The Battle of Normandy

The US 2nd Infantry Division, some 13,000 men strong, was part of the First Army under the orders of Generals Robertson and Bradley. It had landed in Normandy with the US 1st and 29th Divisions, and was heading towards Saint-Vith, in Belgium, then Germany and ultimately Czechoslovakia. The US 2nd Division was known as *Indianhead* in reference to our black badge adorned with the white star of Texas and an Indian's profile. Our motto was 'Second to None'. At the beginning of the war some GIs also wore the badge on their helmets, but the emblems, too easy to spot, were dangerous and so were quickly removed, otherwise the GIs ran the risk of being easy targets.

Several days after the landing at Omaha Beach, nearly all members of the division were present. On 8 June, only a few hours after our landing, we were riding toward stabilized ground. We were at once apprehensive and impatient to know our first mission. Since boarding the landing craft where I'd climbed into my jeep, I still hadn't walked on dry land. Upon arrival in Formigny, I finally set foot on French soil and reported to Colonel Donald P. Christensen, head of the G2 (2nd Bureau) of the 2nd Infantry Division HQ.

There were four sections at the head of each division: G1, Personnel, who assigned soldiers to operation; G2, Military Intelligence, who prepared the operation; G3, Training, who determined the number of men and vehicles required for the operation; G4, Supply and Transportation, who provided material resources.

Emblem of the US 2ⁿᵈ Infantry Division, showing the Indianhead. (Dargols Family Archive)

The division's intelligence unit was meant to go beyond the front-lines in occupied territory. My team acted like a free agent within the division. We operated in this sector to lay the groundwork for the infantry attacks that allowed the villages to be liberated. Unlike the other GIs who weren't allowed to enter occupied territory or to fraternize with the French, among whom there might be collaborationists, I was required to enter villages to gather as much information as possible on German positions. To quote Napoleon: 'A good observer in the right place at the right moment is worth an army corps'. In 1914, some headway was made in that field: the Germans flew *aerostats* (Zeppelins) above French lines, which were connected to the ground via a telephone cable, allowing the Germans to adjust their artillery's fire. In 1944, an attack couldn't be planned or launched without a minimum level of reconnaissance on the enemy. We needed more and more intelligence, mobility and visibility over the Nazi troops.

As an intelligence officer, my mission was to provide reports as comprehensive as possible on the enemy troops we were facing: the composition of units, their whereabouts, works, morale, objectives, but also their weaponry, ammunition depots and fuel stocks. Speaking fluent French made it easier for me to collect information that would be used to decide whether our units were to advance and attack, or instead bypass German positions.

Alongside the path running parallel to the sea and facing the enemy, GIs were lying in prone positions on the ground: aligned a few meters apart, they pointed their rifles forwards, ready to shoot.

Colonel Christensen described my mission:

Lieutenant Colonel Christensen, US 2nd Infantry Division. Photograph taken in the village of Guivapas, Brittany, France, 18 September 1944. (Dargols Family Archive)

> '*Sergeant Dargols.*'
> '*Sir, yes Sir.*'
> '*The front-line is stabilized. The enemy faces us several hundred meters towards Trévières. You will leave all your personal belongings with a comrade in the event that you are made prisoner. Leave letters, photos, any documents you have with you. You will be leaving with an MP in your jeep and going beyond the front-line in order to interrogate and obtain the intelligence we need. You know what to ask, you've been trained for that. All we need is answers.*'

> *He rounded off the talk with:* '*You need to make sure that the intelligence you gather is reliable and corroborated. You have two hours to return the same way you went, otherwise we'll assume you were made prisoner or worse.*'

Deep down I thought, 'Why isn't he going there himself?!'

From now on I was on my own to carry out orders. And that is how 'my' battle of Normandy started.

Bernard in Normandy, July 1944. (Dargols Family Archive)

I was scared: I would need to put into practice all that I'd been taught during my months of training at Camp Ritchie. At the time I still thought my role would consist of informing the French people, or questioning them in a secluded office somewhere, but that turned to be far from the truth: I was to go beyond the front line, leaving the infantry GIs behind where they would wait for us to return with the intelligence they needed to advance.

I left for the front line with an MP, my brain still awash in the fear of our first steps on French soil. I showed my pass to the soldiers stationed on our way. My duties provided all manner of prerogatives. Once in Formigny, I spotted the largest farms and houses in order to interrogate their owners. These buildings were generally the most likely to have accommodated German soldiers. I had two hours to gather as much information as possible.

Fear never left me. The enemy could just as well be 500 meters or 5 kilometers ahead of us. The Germans could be advancing at the very moment we were interrogating civilians. If a German soldier happened to step out of a farmhouse, my mission wasn't to engage in fighting but to shoot and 'get the hell out'. The goal of these missions was to collect reliable intelligence and to minimize casualties among civilians, as well as our own troops. If I was captured, I'd been ordered to disclose only my name, rank and serial number, and absolutely nothing else. Even so, the badge on my left sleeve—the well-known Indianhead— would have given me away as a member of the US 2nd Infantry Division. Luckily, no such thing happened.

On account of the allied bombings that had been carried out to beat back the enemy and facilitate our landing, I was apprehensive about meeting French civilians: the bombings had seriously affected Normandy, destroying villages and inflicting many casualties. But despite the massive extent of the damage, the moment I met the French was unforgettable, truly powerful. When we approached civilians, farmers mostly, in what was in fact a No Man's Land, in the first place came amazement, often followed by tears of joy. People didn't quite know if I was American or French: my jeep was *La Bastille*, I was wearing

Bernard and his jeep La Bastille. Thierry McCormick is sat behind him, at his typewriter. Near Cerisy-la-Forêt, Normandy, July, 1944. (Dargols Family Archive)

a US Army uniform with the MII armband and IndianHead badge, but I spoke perfect French, with a Parisian accent.

They would grill me! Generally, some Normans would stop before the jeep and surround us until someone dragged us inside a house saying 'Come in and how about a wee drink, gentlemen!' And a bottle cork would pop. The French were saving their precious Calvados (apple brandy) for Victory day. I'd reward the kids with chocolate or chewing gum and, the ultimate gift, I'd let them climb in the jeep for a few minutes, which they hugely enjoyed. In Normandy, on the 50th anniversary of D-Day, I was seventy-four and a man in his sixties approached me: 'I remember, Bernard, when you arrived in Bérigny with the first GIs and gave me some chocolate.' He wasn't even fifteen at the time. It was very moving for me to see him again fifty years later.

However, as the moment's emotion subsided, I'd remember my mission and ask a multitude of questions. The villagers were keen to help us and very cooperative. We needed to know if the Germans who had occupied the building had a badge—in order to identify their unit—how many there were and whether they seemed old or not: the older soldiers would more readily surrender, whereas the young ones were determined to keep on fighting re-

Bernard interrogating French civilians. The document he's holding has been censored by the army. Normandy, 2 August 1944. (Dargols Family Archive)

gardless. I would ask them to describe the Germans' behaviour, whether they seemed in good spirits, when they woke up and came back, what they would do during the day. Once I obtained the information, I would have to corroborate it with other civilians to ensure the intelligence was reliable. The slightest detail could change the course of the division's advance.

We would then need to make our way back using the same route as on our way in, and as fast as possible report back to Colonel Christensen, in person in case of emergency. As very few soldiers went beyond the front-line, our GI comrades could have mistaken us for the enemy if we didn't use the same roads to get in and out, and if they hadn't been warned of our return. Upon our return at headquarters, Thierry McCormick was in charge of typing up our reports. The whole process allowed us to inform our division about the Germans' positions and course—some farmers having shown us in which direction they left. I would also report the location of the enemy's fuel depots which I had come to know

Bernard Dargols interrogating a French civilian. Normandy, August 1944. (Dargols Family Archive)

of.[1] It was crucial to destroy them: military vehicles required a lot of fuel. I also gathered information on the location of nearby stores and ammunition depots, and also where roads were mined. I had quickly learned that the Germans spent a sizeable amount of time on placing mines and other obstacles on roads. Engineers and mine-clearing experts then went on site to neutralize the explosives.

These forays occurred daily. Under Colonel Christensen's orders pointing me to certain villages, I also went where I thought I could gather useful knowledge. On each incursion, my heart-rate soared. At any moment, I might come face to face with one or several Germans prepared to open fire. Not focusing on fear allowed me to keep moving. I thought two of us in the jeep would be less easy to spot than a whole troop. Little by little I grew accustomed to these quick trips into occupied territory. I always hoped the enemy was far away

From left to right: Hans Namuth, an IPW agent and Bernard, on the back of a military truck. Normandy, June 1944. (Dargols Family Archive)

and as far as possible from the village where I was meant to question some inhabitants, but twice we came face to face with Germans. They seemed more afraid than we were. I opened fire and we rushed away.

We moved from village to village. The French people, so keen to provide information, spontaneously came to us and were of precious help. We liberated the village of Trévières on 10 June. We were the first to arrive there, our baptism by fire wiped out the German defence but also wreaked havoc in the village: few houses remained standing. In addition, to erase all traces of their presence, the Germans had set fire to whatever had survived the bombings.

From Trévières the division set forth in the direction of Cerisy-la-Forêt, by way of Molay-Littry. On the road we were instructed to never advance in groups, but to 'spread out.'

A few tanks opened the way. The infantry GIs marched by the roadside, some riding trucks. McCormick and I drove the jeep slowly. On our way we heard some mines explode in the distance. As we drew close to a danger zone the convoy stopped. Some GIs, veteran base-ball players, pitched hand grenades with strength and dexterity that impressed me. Once the front-line was stabilized McCormick and I went to Molay-Littry and Cerisy-la-Forêt and returned two hours later with the intelligence gathered to identify German positions and mined roads. Typically, tanks would stay located at the corner of a meadow to avoid detection, waiting there for the signal to get going.

Once in Cerisy-la-Forêt the division's headquarters settled near the village, at La Boulaye to be precise. There we waited for reinforcement in men, ammunition and fuel in order to carry on. Cerisy was not a voluntary stop. German defences were ferocious and there were 540 fatalities between 12 and 13 June. US reconnaissance troops actively patrolled the roads of Cerisy-la-Forêt. We knew the woods surrounding the village harboured enemy fuel and ammunition depots. During the four days of combat the division had advanced 25 kilometers inland, one attack following the other, and dozens of prisoners were taken and interrogated by the IPW.

US Army trucks transporting German prisoners. Summer 1944. (Dargols Family Archive)

A new mission awaited me. Colonel Christensen indicated: 'You will go see Doctor Stanislas Champain the moment you enter Cerisy-la-Forêt.' Doctor Champain ran the village's only pharmacy. He was the first resistant I was meant to interrogate and this turned out to be my most significant memory. I found the pharmacy and asked to talk to him, to which a woman all in black answered: 'Unfortunately, Doctor Champain was killed yesterday during a bombing.' She was his daughter, but it was me she had to comfort. I was devastated. I very much counted on this meeting. She didn't however ask me for its reason, which I wouldn't have given her in any event. Seeing my emotion, she fetched me some paregoric[14] from the the back room, telling me: 'mix it with a little water and you'll have made yourself a pastis,[15] it'll do you good.' In 2002 I met Doctor Champain's son during a ceremony in memory of the war victims. It was emotional.

I had unearthed an oil lamp which we used at night. When inland we slept under a nylon tent. The dark and quiet nights stoked our fear when the rumble of a tank drew closer and closer. It only took us a few seconds to determine if it was one of ours or one of theirs approaching. Nights were short.

I told my father: 'We're used to the sound of bombs whistling above the woods nearby. Launched in the direction of the Germans, some fly so close to us that they terrify us. We have fixed up a lean-to for shelter.'

Gigantic kitchens were set up in the nearby field. Meals were plentiful and we could always get second servings. We were provided with almost unlimited supplies of chocolate and cigarettes. During missions and forays into villages we ate K and C rations. C ration was a kind of beef stew with vegetables and we reheated the canned rations in our helmets filled with boiling hot water. K rations were eaten cold. They were wrapped in a watertight cardboard and were therefore weatherproof. They were made up of chocolate, candy, chewing-

Thierry McCormick on the left and Bernard Dargols on the right. Near Cerisy-la-Forêt, July 1944. (Dargols Family Archive)

Kitchen installations in a field. Guipavas, Brittany, September 1944. (Dargols Family Archive)

gum and fruit-paste, stodgy but very nourishing and filled with vitamins, to be chewed on over a long period of time.

The division carried on to cross the Elle river on 13 June and liberated the villages, pushing back the more or less unyielding Germans. The battle at Saint-Georges-d'Elle was especially tough. The village was first liberated, then taken back by the Germans, before being retaken again thanks to the 2nd Division's counter-attack. Not far away, the German Panzerdivision *Das Reich*, after killing 642 civilians in Ouradour,[16] was approaching St-Lô.

Tired and dirty after several days of fighting, we could doubtless have been nosed out by the Germans. One day near Saint-Georges-d'Elle, and close to Hill 192, a surprise awaited us. Portable showers, a dozen meters long, had been pitched and camouflaged in the fields. Shedding our clothes, we got in from one side and out from the other after being passed under hot water. We enjoyed the pleasure of feeling clean and having new combat uniforms.

Bernard Dargols holding a mess-kit, right next to a minefield near Cerisy-la-Forêt., July 1944. (Dargols Family Archive)

Cut off from any communication with my family for several weeks, I wrote my first letter after the landing to my father, who had no idea I was in France.

> *Somewhere in France, 22 June 1944*
>
> *Dear Papa,*
>
> *Before writing a longer air-mail to you, I want to tell you that everything is alright with me and that you must not worry, as I have told you many times.*
>
> *Yesterday, I received your D-Day V-mail and even if I knew you were safe in New York, I would not have changed places with you.*
>
> *After all the waiting we've done, all our family in fact, it is now that you will have to be the most patient. (...)*

Continue sending me anything that can be eaten: chocolate, canned pineapple, sardines, etc.

I don't have to tell you that I get along very well with the population here, as if I were a Frenchman. They are so surprised when they hear me talk!

I'll finish now. One day, this radio you are listening to will let you know the best news ever: Peace.

Kisses to Marcel, Simon and to you.

Bernard

I would send airmail letters or V-mails, whose size was the smallest possible.[17]

I wrote whenever I had a few minutes and received a bulk of letters every two weeks or so: Françoise's daily letters, and those from my father and brothers. We exchanged news from everybody, but in the main these letters were meant to reassure each other on our morale and health. Simply reading that 'everything was fine' was comforting, despite knowing that we were protecting each other from the difficulties we encountered in our respective situations.

I couldn't imagine ever losing this war. The constant and flawless optimism my parents had passed on provided me with enough energy and hope to continue my mission. My goal was to get it over with and that we all be reunited. I again wrote my father, from 'somewhere in France' without being allowed to provide details about our advance:

In France, Friday, 30 June 1944

Papa,

Yesterday, I was invited for dinner by a farmer and his wife. It was my first meal in France and my first piece of bread in five and a half years. All of which was washed down with a bottle of St Emilion, then cider, then black coffee and a glass of Calvados to round it all off. The Calva was so strong that it made your helmet rise ten inches above your

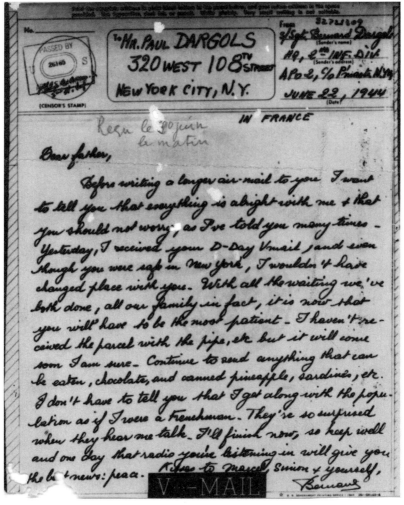

V-mail from Bernard to his father dated 22 June 1944. As letter were censored by the American Army, Bernard was only allowed to give his location as, 'In France'. (Dargols Family Archive)

head. We started with an excellent soup, then veal with green peas from the garden and some seasoned lettuce. It was unbelievable.

Now and then, the sound of cannons made the women jump and I felt the house might crumble. We spoke about a thousand things.

The news could reach you with a certain delay but it got to us fast: Cherbourg was liberated the day before yesterday. Things will probably move faster from now on. Conditions of life in the villages we liberate are getting better and better. Little by little normal life is returning now that the fear of the Germans has disappeared.

All is well. Please don't worry.

I hope we'll all be home for Christmas [in English in the letter].

A few days after the landing, a GI from the Signal Corps, the army's photographic department, solicited me for a photo which would represent the good Franco-American relationship. He asked me to find a woman farmer in clogs who would, if possible, carry a yoke with a bucket on each end. 'Find another GI and pretend to help the young woman fill her buckets with water.' The other GI in the photograph was called William L. Stanley. The photographer found a spot in front of a bread oven in Cerisy-la-Forêt where we posed following his instructions. The photograph, taken on 15 June, ended up featuring on the front page of most US newspapers on 1 July 1944. The 2nd Infantry Division's badge was expunged from the published photography. The division's position could not be revealed but, contrary to my request, my name and location were published. That day Françoise discovered all these front pages with my photo spread out on her bed. She was told, 'You wanted some news from Bernard. Here you go!?' Françoise, who hadn't heard from me for weeks, learned that I was alive and 'somewhere in France.' Some forty years later a journalist from the daily *Ouest-France*, Mr Legoupil, allowed me to meet up again with the woman, Marie-Jeanne Brossard. And once again in front of the bread oven we took the same picture, with much emotion. There, she recalled her mother's apprehension at the time, as she saw her daughter leave with two GIs, asking if she was quite sure that their real purpose was to take a photograph.

GRAM, SATURDAY, JULY 1, 1944.   NY WORLD TELEGRAM

st Clash with GOP Old

Help for the Farmer's Daughter

Two GI Joes are shown helping a French farmer's daughter fetch a couple of pails of water from an army filter truck in Normandy.. The accommodating soldiers are S/Sgt. Bernard Dargols, 320 W. 108th St., New York City (left), and T/5 William L. Stanley, of Houston, Texas.
U. S. Signal Corps Picture from Acme.

From left to right: Marie-Jeanne Brossard, Bernard and William L. Stanley in Cerisy-la-Forêt on 15 June 1944.

In this censored photograph, the emblem of the 2nd Infantry Division has been erased. The picture appeared on the cover of several American newspapers on 1 July 1944. (Dargols Family Archive)

The original version of the same photograph taken by the Signal Corps, before being censored for publication. (Dargols Family Archive)

*Bernard Dargols and Marie-Jeanne Brossard recreating the same photograph
forty years later (1984) in Normandy.* (Dargols Family Archive)

When Françoise wrote me she said that I was lucky to be in France, to which I answered jokingly: 'why, do you think I've been sightseeing?'

The distribution of mail improved by the day and I eagerly waited for a GI yelling 'Mail Call!' when the military truck arrived at the field. Françoise wrote several letters a week; it was marvellous to receive news from my family and friends in the US. During these difficult times, it was wonderfully sustaining. On the other hand, I had next to no news from France.

***

In Molay-Littry, Saint-Jean-des-Baisants, Saint Georges D'Elle and Bérigny we continued to gather intelligence from civilians concerning the occupiers, which we reported back to our superiors. Gradually, owing to my role with the French, I was more in touch with them than with the men in my division. The Normans, in shock, cried with joy when they saw us: finally, their villages were liberated from the enemy. I learned of the tortures and abuse inflicted on the French, who were traumatized by the nightmarish hardships they had endured. The Germans bought food supplies from the farmers, which they would send to their families in Germany. We were strictly prohibited from doing that, to avoid depriving them or the relatives who relied on them, food being a daily concern for all. But we were more than happy to exchange bananas, chocolate, cigarettes or chewing-gum for butter and eggs. The Germans had requisitioned copper, which the French had hid and upon our arrival, copper vases and candelabras suddenly reappeared in houses. They even polished some of our C ration cans and displayed them on their mantelpieces. Our questions were always welcome and so were we.

Some French civilians, without being members of resistance groups, nevertheless helped the Allies. Those who transported messages on their bikes ran the risk of being executed. In Molay-Littry two Resistants didn't hesitate to ride beyond the front-line on their bikes to hand me over some crucial intelligence. Other divisions, such as the 29th, had noted the same thing: the resistance in that sector was sporadic and barely organized. This made sense to us considering the thousands of messages launched a few days before the landing all along the Atlantic coast, which encouraged the civilians to move as far as they could from the coast. Among these civilians, many would doubtless have communicated information just as essential for us.

From village to village the GIs marched in single file on either side of the road. I was lucky to be riding the jeep. One day in late June 1944, an officer shouted, 'Take ten!' We stopped for a routine 10-minute break: each of us would immediately dig a fox-hole, about 6.5 ft by 3 ft wide and 1 ft deep, to duck into and take shelter in the event of an airborne attack. These few moments of respite allowed us to relax and regain enough strength to move on.

The breaks represented for many of us the opportunity to practice pitching our baseballs. As for me, I slipped on my boxing gloves and recalled the words of my teacher, Georges Papin: 'You box using your legs, hit using your body and place using your fists.' On that June day, McCormick and I had just begun throwing a few punches when a jeep drove up to us. Out came a Civil Affairs major who, as we

Bernard in a fox-hole. Normandy, June 1944. (Dargols Family Archive)

stood to attention, asked McCormick to lend him his gloves so as to exchange a few punches with me. It was a rather delicate situation because hitting a superior could have had me court martialed. Straightaway, I noted that the major, although short, was heavier than me. My reach could, however, easily keep him at bay. I let him push me around for a few minutes, but when his punches became painful I couldn't stop myself from letting a violent straight fly to his chin. I had visualized him with a swastika in lieu of his face - so long hierarchy! I feared the worst but he congratulated me. 'Well done,' he said, then 'Good luck Bernard.' It all happened in less than five minutes.

When I was back in Paris I recounted this anecdote to my Gaullist Army friends, who were duly amazed. It was inconceivable in the French Army; officers and privates did not have that kind of relationships. Between us, relationships were respectful but relaxed, especially in the Intelligence Service.

Days went by and missions were carried out. The narrow roads of Normandy quickly proved to be very dangerous. The enormous hedges, high and wide, which lined the paths in these zones of wooded countryside, made it difficult for the division to advance: tanks had a hard time navigating the terrain and the aviation's help was limited by low visibility, worsened by the bad weather. The infantry inched its way hedge after hedge, owing our intrusion its name; the 'Battle of Hedgerows'. The retreating enemy had strung wires, almost invisible, between the trees on either side of the roads. The tactic had caused many wounds among the motorized troops, sometimes even decapitating some GIs, and thousands died before a solution was found. A few days after our arrival in Normandy, our two jeeps were taken to the 'Ordnance', which dealt with the maintenance of vehicles. They seemed to us in good shape and had been checked three days before departure in Cardiff. But they were returned to us equipped with a slanted cornice welded onto the front. Tanks were also fitted with a hedge-breaching device, robust steel blades that sliced the hedges off their base. The hedges thus removed then turned into camouflage for the tanks. This clever invention was the work of Curtis G. Culin who was an engineer and served as a tanker in the 102nd Cavalry Reconnaissance Squadron. On 11 July 1944, Hill 192, whose peak was 192 meters above sea level—hence its name—was taken as part of the 'Battle of Hedgerows', and was a decisive victory which allowed the division to advance towards Bérigny, Saint-Jean-des-Baisants, Vire, Tinchebray, Saint-Lô and Saint-Georges-d'Elle, where the enemy had withdrawn. The hill offered a general view of the landing operations, towards Omaha on one side and Saint-Lô on the other, the 29th Division's sector, which would soon be liberated as well.

Still stationed in Cerisy-la-Forêt we explored the neighbouring villages. I went to Saint-Lô with an MP and together we entered deserted land. In this landscape of desolation, where everything would need to be rebuilt, I noticed a cat meandering among the ruins. The silence was almost deafening. I carried on, aware of the war's terrible consequences. The few houses that hadn't been razed were still burning. Dead animals in the bombed villages gave off a pestilential smell which made us nauseous. We also liberated Saint-Clair-sur-Elle, le Molay-Littry and other villages, all of which are to this day engraved in my memory. Liberating these villages one after the other kept our spirits up; it might even bring me closer to the day when I would finally be reunited with my family.

Bernard Dargols with his jeep. Normandy, June 1944. (Dargols Family Archive)

***

No-Man's-Land. Normandy, June 1944. (Dargols Family Archive)

On 4 July 1944, Independence Day was celebrated in Cerisy's marketplace in the presence of General Robertson (the head of the US 2nd Infantry Division), the village mayor, some local public figures and villagers, and a few GIs. Two days earlier Omar Bradley, who was in charge of the first US Army and Dwight 'Ike' Eisenhower, Commander in Chief of all the Allied armies, had given the 2nd Division a pep talk, from which I extracted a few anecdotes for my father.

> *France, 4 July 1944*
>
> *Dear Papa,*
>
> *Well! Here is Independence Day celebrated in France. All is well. The French people in the village next to ours have decorated their houses with Allied flags for the American national day.*
>
> *Our General made a one-minute speech. We learned with pleasure that Minsk in Poland was liberated. We celebrated with Pernod and a glass of real Champagne. The period is still pro-Nazi but I'm sure it will change soon.*

*Photograph taken on 4 July 1944 for Independence Day in Cerisy-la-Forêt.
General Robertson is on the right, in the foreground, and Mr Godin, Mayor of
Cerisy-la-Forêt, is in the centre. To the Mayor's right, Lieutenant Christophe
(Gaullist Army) is speaking to Hans Namuth. Behind the Mayor, McCormick
and Bernard can be seen in the crowd.* (Dargols Family Archive)

*Sometimes, we see Citroën vehicles on the road with the
white Allied star, appropriated by the American Army.
(And I've noticed that French dogs bark with the same
accent as American dogs.)*

Everything is going well for me for the moment.

Bernard

PS: I'm smoking a pipe right now.

Every day dozens of people would gather on the marketplace to listen to the news broadcast from the loudspeaker on an American truck. The Nazis, in their haste to leave, had left behind the TSF[18] radios they'd confiscated from the villagers and stock-piled in the town hall. We had them returned to their rightful owners, but power hadn't been restored yet and the radios were useless.

One day in July, the truck was playing the French, American and English anthems as well as the new Russian song, to the people's applause. A few minutes after it left I saw French youngsters lead seven women, twenty to forty-five years of age, towards a carriage door. I immediately recognized the women as having dated German officers. An hour later they came out entirely shaved. We were very impressed by this score-settling among French people and stayed out of it. Later I had to interrogate around forty of these women, who we dubbed 'horizontal collaborators'. All worked for the Germans as waitresses, cleaners or typists. For the most part, their husbands were prisoners in Germany. One of them was twenty. As I searched her purse I found a social security card from the 4th arrondissement of Paris. We were from the same neighbourhood. How could she have lowered herself to that? I was in a terrible rage.

Some French men had been in hiding for months, years sometimes, to escape the STO imposed by the Germans. Many French people seemed 'bewildered' by the German propaganda, as if poisoned by the near endless occupation. Shortly after liberating their villages, I would ask their opinion about Pétain: some would answer, 'He's a great man who served France very well.' 'What about De Gaulle? I asked 'Well yeah! We know him, he's a general, but Pétain is better.' Anti-Semitism still existed and only much later, after the war, did the many French 'Righteous Among the Nations' come to be known. They had saved innocent lives at the risk of their own.

The US Army planned to have the collaborationist mayors jailed and to temporarily replace them with GIs from the Civil Affairs division until the free France government would take over. The provisional administration was to be called AMGOT, Allied Military Government in Occupied Territories. But De Gaulle vehemently opposed this decision, which he deemed intrusive. As a result, many mayors whose views had been amenable to the occupier were maintained in their position. I had held high hopes that the Gaullist Army would remove these shady elements from public life. I was devastated by these decisions. I believed we might win the war, but what kind of peace would we recover?

We had been in Cerisy-la-Forêt for several weeks now and some of us were actually sleeping in farms. I remember that for my part, I slept over a hairdresser's shop, which no longer exists. Alarming information was reaching us through civilians: the enemy was engaged in unusual activities and their preparation suggested a surprise counter-attack. I still had in mind the devastation in Saint-Georges-d'Elle and Trévières. The consequences would be tragic if the same were to happen

Lieutenant Wrenn, in front of the destroyed Albert Louppe bridge in Brittany, near Brest, 1944. (Dargols Family Archive)

in Cerisy-la-Forêt. Without alerting the population to the potential danger, McCormick and I resolved to patrol the village. Side by side, armed, calm and reassuring, we didn't let our attitude betray the potential of imminent danger. The counter-attack never happened and our division decided to launch the breakthrough which would lead the Nazis to collapse.

When back-up finally arrived, the 2nd Division resumed its advance towards Falaise then the north-east, thus marking the end of the Battle of Normandy.

Brittany had already been liberated, but to my great despair, and while my comrades were moving closer to Paris, I was sent to one of the Wehrmacht's final pockets of resistance in the Atlantic region, the city of Brest, which remained in the grip of the German Army.

CHAPTER 6

The Atlantic Pocket of Brest

In early August, in the village of Tinchebray, we were ordered to pack up and head towards Brittany within the hour. We were leaving Normandy behind us, after being there for around two months. We left by night for a very long trip, the convoy comprising of dozens of military jeeps and trucks. In order to avoid detection, the rear lights of the vehicles were camouflaged, emitting only the slightest sliver of light. We had to fight off sleep. I recall struggling to keep my eyes open by staring, for kilometers on end, at the lights of the jeep opening the way for us. Along the roads, I caught more glimpses of devastated villages. Only ruins remained. German cars, skewed and sprayed with bullets, were abandoned; a German tank set on fire was still smoking. A German soldier had tried, in vain, to escape and only a blackened leg stuck out from the passenger door. Also burnt were two camouflage-painted Parisian city buses, which lay toppled over by the curb. The Germans had most likely requisitioned them to transport their troops. I recognized a town I had cycled through seven years earlier with my Youth Hostel Association pals.

As I was driving, my thoughts returned to Normandy, to the emotion of its population wounded by bombings and years of enduring the occupation. The convoy came to a halt at a level crossing. A brand-new train, impressively long, was pulled by two locomotives. The Allies' white star and the letters USA flashed on the dozens of wagons that passed in front of us.

Destroyed buildings in Gouesnou (Brittany), September 1944. (Dargols Family Archive)

It was the first time I saw an American train in France, and it was so good to hear its whistle!

The convoy stopped near Landerneau. Straightaway, following instructions, we covered the jeep and trailer with a camouflage net, dug a foxhole to take shelter in the event of an attack and pitched our tent. At dawn, we resumed our trip towards Brest. Our convoy was by no means inconspicuous. Frenzied and overjoyed children would sing and dance. As we passed by, men raised their arm and formed the V for Victory with their fingers, others saluted; others still held out glasses of wine or cider. Women and young girls would scream and yell 'Vive l'Amérique! Vive l'Amérique',[1] and blow kisses and throw flowers at us. Others, their arms laden with baskets, offered us eggs the moment the convoy stopped for a few minutes. I felt like I was dreaming.

We set up our offices in Gouesnou, in deserted elementary schools or kindergartens. Alongside the children's drawings

Bernard and a FFI agent in Landerneau (Brittany), September 1944.
(Dargols Family Archive)

and murals that decorated the walls, dozens of posters and photographs displaying Pétain seemed to taunt us. We hastened to rip them down and trample them as soon as we arrived, because the man who claimed to sacrifice his life to the French people had, in fact, deeply wounded the country. We discovered that textbooks had been expunged and some of their pages ripped out. I recall that in one school, riddled with shrapnel holes and all its window shattered, only a wall clock still worked, in a Surrealist-like scene.

In the school yard, MPs holding their sub-machine guns kept 100 German prisoners under surveillance. Each was to be questioned for around an hour by the Interrogation of Prisoners of War section (IPW). I walked by them and scrutinized the ever-so-ordinary faces of these defeated enemies; each had a photograph of Hitler with him. For me, it would have been strange to carry a photograph of Roosevelt on me. This is how I described them in a letter to my father: 'They were skinny,

The village of Gouesnou (Brittany) following the bombings, September 1944.
(Dargols Family Archive)

bald and short. They were gathered together and seemed awfully well-behaved, but worried.' The German soldiers were subjected to such propaganda that they would ask us if New York city still existed—Goebbels had them believe that, among other things, the Nazis had bombed the city.

For them the war was over. They were to be sent to England or the US. We continued our way towards the village of Guipavas, a few kilometers north-east of Brest, where battles fighting the Germans were severe. In Guipavas American military trucks, crowned with the large white star, were filled with pathetic German prisoners whose arrogance had vanished. They arrived by the thousand. It was unbelievable. They would sooner be prisoners of the Americans than be sent to the extreme conditions of the Russian front. They weren't, for instance, equipped for the arctic cold. As prisoners of the American Army they were protected by the Geneva convention, meaning they were fed and shipped to prisoner camps in the US. When

The 'cave' where prisoners coming from Brest were collected. Guipavas,
18 September 1944. (Dargols Family Archive)

Sergeant Haller (IPW) in front of German prisoners in Brittany, 1944.
(Dargols Family Archive)

Convoy of German prisoners travelling from Brest towards Guipavas,
September 1944. (Dargols Family Archive)

the trucks passed through the village to go behind the lines, the
villagers would drop everything to holler '*bastards*', or '*dirty*
Krauts', as if to relieve themselves.

I continued my mission by traipsing all over Brest and its
region to gather intelligence from civilians. At the city entrance
we passed by a destroyed Citroën factory, of which no more than
a fragile carcass remained, on the brink of collapse. I entered
another factory that produced aeroplane parts for the Germans
and spotted a 1942 phone book for Paris. I couldn't help myself
from looking up the section 'rue des francs-bourgeois': there
it was, the advert for 'Dargols (Paul), sewing machines'. The
family store and its bustling activity felt like ages ago, but I was
still hoping for the requisite authorisations to travel to Paris,
when possible, and when the city would finally be liberated.

In Brittany, my fellow soldiers were astonished to see women
dressed in black with their traditional white headgear. We would
meet others wearing a turban to conceal their shaved head.

Ruins of the Citroën warehouse on the outskirts of Brest, September 1944.
(Dargols Family Archive)

The GIs were baffled by the *pissotières* (small stand-alone structures housing public urinals). Some would stop, hesitate and, after a final analysis, give up in front of this French curiosity. We weren't allowed to take pictures: Hans Namuth, a professional photographer in his civilian life, never lost a chance to flout the rule.

Mail remained very irregular, but I kept up exchanges with my father, who was still in New York:

In France, 30 August 1944.

Dear Papa

I've been in France for about 2 months at least. I don't have the patience to describe my departure from Britain and my arrival in France. Another day maybe.

But I'm taking advantage of a few moments off to write the main events of these last few days.

To answer your last letter about 'the souvenirs I received from theses bastards', it was just a silk scarf and a Nazi eagle which Nazi soldiers wore on their tunics.

We received two shots from the medics. The last injections were 6 months ago.

A few days ago, I returned way back behind the front line. One of the the village bigwigs, who we knew was a member of the PSF (French Nazi collaborators party), took advantage of the situation and asked to join De Gaulle's forces as soon as the Americans arrived. He was accepted as a first lieutenant and can you imagine I should now have to salute him?

I passed through more than ten villages. In my division's sector, one of the toughest if not the toughest, you can count on the fingers of both hands the number of houses which haven't been hit. The undertakers are overworked.

The more we move forward in the direction of the capital, the less milk, butter and meat can be found.

Here, some movie theaters, due to lack of electricity, are powered with gas. Large veal côtelettes (first-rate) are sold for 60 francs at the butcher's.

I spent the last 8 days in a village with a family who were forced to house German soldiers who had wanted some rest after fighting in Russia. One of the German officers told them that he had entered a farm with his team to stay overnight, and that he had been quite surprised to be so well received by this Russian peasant family. The next day, the farm had been emptied and [he found] his team killed on the second floor. Since then he was 'a little' scared of the Russians.

Some Krauts around here, who left shortly before we got here, behaved liked real savages. Girls, and children also, still wake up in the middle of the night, terrified: the Nazis are back. Just to tell you their state of mind!

There is no doubt the Yankees are quite popular with French women! Those who wanted to go out with Germans did so in secret.

At the center of the village I spoke to a man who hid with farmers for a year and a half to escape the law, which was forcing him to go work in Germany.

One day, when I returned to the village, the Germans started bombing. There were no Allied soldiers in the village and my room faced the church. The first bomb fell on the church. Women were in a panic about the children and even the dogs and cats seemed to have gone mad. The FFI troops took the situation in hand. A few more bombs fell, killing and wounding several people, but I didn't bat an eyelid. Many bombs in fact fell without exploding.

The FTP (Francs Tireurs et partisans) are nice fellows too. They've all adopted American names: either Freddy, Charlie, etc. and that's how they like to be called.

Nazi soldiers slept in farmers' homes, but to us it's strictly forbidden. Our HQ and my small team were in an abandoned school. The first thing I did was to tear off three large portraits of Maréchal Pétain which were decorating a small classroom.

The 'Frisés' gentlemen, in their haste to leave France where they had lived so well, left a huge amount of stuff on the roadside.

We got hold of a new German trailer which we attached to the back of our jeep. The only problem was repainting it and putting the white Allied star on it instead.

I was granted a special authorization to sleep in the village. I chose an old lady who already had 8 people under her roof, only women (she has 2 daughters and the others are a family of refugees, staying here for the time being). She cooks amazingly well. They nearly fainted when they drank some real coffee (yours) and tasted several of the little things you had sent. I have a clean room and office and a swell bed with the occasional flea (that's France, right?) But the DDT powder the army provides is remarkable. I think that a pinch of it would kill a cow. The strangest thing is that a German officer was sleeping in the very same bed five days ago.

Some soldiers say hello to me. When I tell them that I don't know them, they answer 'yes of course, but we know you, you gave us a lecture in England!'

Here I saw my first USO open- air show,[19] it lasted an hour, with a band, etc.. It was in a field. Cows came over to watch, with a baffled look, at all this blowing of trombones and trumpets.

And there it is. That's all loads of fun, but I'm so far away from the people I want to be with. But I'll do anything, for sure, to see Maman. All I want for Christmas is a small victory.

Bernard.

In the month of August 1944, two French officers, Christophe and Fouquet, accompanied us in our forays. On the front line I unearthed a Peugeot 301, used by the Germans and then abandoned, which was well-hidden inside a barn. After careful scrutiny to make sure it wasn't a trap - the Germans had a habit of setting booby traps around doors and windows of houses - I tried out the car It was in perfect shape, and I handed it over to officer Fouquet. As I sniffed around, I chanced upon a barrel of Calvados, which I immediately transferred into dozens of bottles using a rubber tube, and then distributed around in generous servings.

At the end of August 1944, I was told that Paris had been liberated. Later, I found the letter my mother had sent to my father and Marcel in New York:

My very dear ones, liberation! Liberation! The word in itself really evokes such a recent past of coercion and retribution, but also of hope in a future that will make life

Standing, from left to right: Thierry McCormick, a Forces Françaises Libres lieutenant and Bernard, with Sergeant Brod at the front. Brittany, September 1944. (Dargols Family Archive)

Bernard Dargols sitting on a Peugeot 301 that was found in a barn. Brittany, August 1944. (Dargols Family Archive)

worth living. The liberation of Paris was carried out in such a grandiose way and at such surprising speed that we were utterly stunned. Then the parade through Paris of Allied troops welcomed with delirious happiness and elation! In truth I hardly dared leave the house, in the hope of a visit from English or American soldiers. I wasn't mistaken and the first to come in a jeep was Eddie Coleman to give me some news of Bernard, whom he was sorry to leave.

From New York, my father answered my mother:

Dear Little Yetta,

You have waited for nearly six years, and often you thought this moment would never come. But everything has changed. A Russian proverb says: 'Someday we'll have a party in our street, too.' The day has finally arrived.

Paul

The liberation of Paris made everyone very optimistic about the future; even so, for us GIs the war was still ongoing. Thanks to the liberation of Paris we could communicate again with my mother. My father would send me parcels of coffee, tobacco and other supplies, which I'd promptly forward on to her. As for me, although the army provided for all my needs, I did request sardines and chocolate in each of my letters. On the other hand, my mother, who was caring for my grandparents, was in need of everything. Despite her reassuring letters, rationing and persecution of Jews were no longer limited to only men. Women and the elderly were just as likely to be rounded up for arrest. Photos of my mother wearing mourning clothes betrayed the hard times she was experiencing, even if she didn't talk about them.

My motivation increased. Upon our arrival in Brest, our office was set up close to barrack occupied by the FFI,[20] with whom we cooperated very efficiently. These FFI were haphazardly dressed, in civilian clothes, in British or American uniforms, or half civilian/half soldier outfits. Among other things, their actions were aimed at disrupting German communication lines.

Bernard Dargols with an FFI agent, 1944. (Dargols Family Archive)

They were armed and were of precious help to us. It was my first encounter with French members of the fighting resistance and I was impressed with their courage: they played with danger like a child with her doll. They painted names on the few civilian cars they had at their disposal, and the first car I saw sported enormous letters reading 'love deprived'.

In my jeep, and with Master Sergeant Haller who was part of a team charged with interrogating prisoners of war, I was required to make several incursions into occupied Brest. Our first foray consisted of finding the German Headquarters, which we knew were located in a bank. Quiet and extremely alert, we walked through a vast and semi-deserted square in Brest, with our sub-machine guns. The town was one large pile of rubble and the *Kommandantur* was partly destroyed. Armed and resolute, we scaled the few stairs that led inside the building: it was empty. We went to the second floor to inspect the offices and the prevailing mess suggested its occupants had

Bernard Dargols with his machine gun. Brest, August 1944. (Dargols Family Archive)

fled in all haste. It was clear that as the personnel had deserted the place, they had taken as much as possible with them. There was nothing left. Not a single document or note, nothing. Just a handful of useless papers that were scattered across the floor.

Brest was still in the hands of the Germans and the situation required extreme vigilance. The air force was less prevalent than in Normandy, but the town hadn't yet been retaken. I typically would seek out school teachers and headmasters in order to collect intelligence, but here the inhabitants spontaneously approached us to show us where the Gestapo was. The Breton people were very helpful. As in Normandy, I obtained the necessary intelligence about the Nazi positions, the whereabouts of their ammunition and fuel depots, as well as the roads they had mined. After two hours in the field I returned to headquarters to report back to Colonel Christensen.

A few days later, the battleground was surrounded and the Germans officially capitulated. Convinced that the place was now completely free of the enemy, I left my machine gun in the jeep and took up my camera instead. Alone in the ruins, I drew close to the buildings lining the deserted main square. As I peered into openings, I realised the basements were inhabited. I stopped in front of a concrete basement-shelter

The former Kommandantur building in Brest. August 1944. (Dargols Family Archive)

which the Germans had shored up. I leaned over and saw, through the basement window bars, a German soldier who looked frightened to death.

Quickly collecting myself I yelled in my very basic German, '*Warfen Lüger!*' then '*Raus!*' ('Throw your gun and get out!') With fear in his heart, he complied. I had him place his hands on his head to body search him, and confiscated the huge parachutist knife he was carrying. He was now walking ahead of me with his hands up and a gun to his back. This is how I led him across the deserted town square, before handing him over to an MP. He then realised the only weapon I had was his revolver. The other GIs had a good laugh when they learned how I had 'busted' him. I never left without my gun afterwards.

He was my one and only direct prisoner throughout the whole war. Wouldn't my mother be happy to know that I had never killed anybody? Although, indirectly, many were arrested and killed owing to the information I collected. But I also prevented many useless bombings of GIs and French civilians.

***

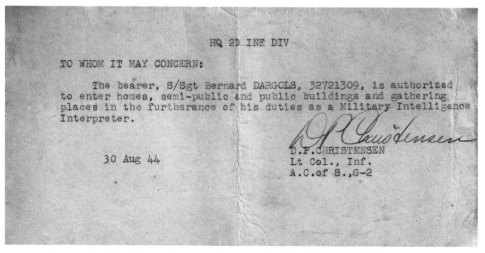

HQ 2D INF DIV

TO WHOM IT MAY CONCERN:

The bearer, S/Sgt Bernard DARGOLS, 32721309, is authorized to enter homes, semi-public and public buildings and gathering places in the furtherance of his duties as a Military Intelligence Interpreter.

D.F. CHRISTENSEN
Lt Col., Inf.
A.C.of S.,G-2

30 Aug 44

Pass authorizing Bernard to enter homes and public places as a MII agent. August 1944. (Dargols Family Archive)

In early September, I met a trucker heading for Paris. Now that the route from Brittany to Paris was back under Allied control, his company had resumed traffic to the capital. In a few words I told him my story and asked him to call on my mother, who I hadn't had direct news from for several years. I entrusted him with a letter and a parcel to be given to her in person. I also asked him to tell her I was in good health, and that one way or the other I would make my way back to her at home:

France, 1 September 1944

Dear Maman.

I've just been told that truck drivers leave from here with loads of vegetables for Paris. One of them agreed to bring you this letter. I wanted to let you know how much I hope you and the rest of the family who are with you are in good health.

I never told you that I was in the American Army as a staff sergeant, in a section where my French is indispensable. I feel in great shape. Don't worry about me, trust me.

I get letters from Marcel and Simon who are in very good health and I also write to them twice a week.

You can imagine that I'm doing everything I can to come see you all but [being in] the army isn't synonymous with freedom. You can write to me by giving your letter to any US soldier. Write your letter in English, keep it short and put it in an open envelope so it can be read by an officer for possible censorship.

Many kisses,

Bernard.

The truck driver was due back seven days later in Landerneau and the week of waiting was truly unbearable for me. He returned with a note and a photo of my mother, who was deeply moved when she had read my letter.

On 18 September 1944, Brest was officially liberated after weeks of offensives that had started on 25 August. During these weeks of military operations 37,832 Germans were arrested by the VIII Army, among which 11,000 were captured by the US 2nd Division.

***

Our mission in Brittany was finished. Paris was free, but the war wasn't over yet. The Division left on 26 September for Saint-Vith in the Ardennes, where it would remain until 12 December 1944. As for me, I received the order to travel, as always with my jeep, to Le Vesinet (10 miles from Paris), more precisely to the Pavillon des Ibis. The place had been occupied by the Germans since 1940, but we had driven them out and this vast structure now accommodated our troops. We rested there between assignments. Posted on the little bridge at the Pavilion's entrance, I spent an entire night as sentry on the lookout for foreign intrusions. Today the Pavilion has become a fancy restaurant.

This is when I was given special permission to go and visit my family. Seeing Paris after six years of absence didn't arouse the emotion I had expected: after Normandy and Brittany, I anticipated it to be much more damaged by war than it was. In fact, there were few soldiers in the streets and only some MPs.

Lieutenant Wrenn drove me home. When I arrived at 8, rue des Francs-bourgeois, the shutters of our shop were pulled down and I opened the heavy carriage door to park the jeep in the building's courtyard. The concierge was almost scared to death, but recognised me and I asked her to warn my mother. Our neighbors, the pharmacist, were home and observed us. I ran up the three stories and came face to face with my mother. She looked exhausted. We embraced for a very long time. My emotion was immense after such a long separation and the dread of knowing her to be in danger. When she saw me she said: 'I wept too much before, I can't any more.' The long-awaited moment of our reunion had finally arrived and remains unforgettable.

She told me about the death of my two grandmothers and that her father, Grandfather Bloom, had been arrested in March 1944 and sent to Drancy at the age of 85. My mother had moved heaven and earth to have him released, even going to the Swiss consulate to hand them his British passport. In July 1944, after months of administrative procedures and four months of detention in Drancy, he was transferred to the Rothschild Foundation hospital where, although not free, he was spared from deportation to the extermination camps. He was discharged a few days after the Liberation. I later learned of the risks taken by some staff members of the hospital: they had delivered groundless medical certificates in order to have young children released from Drancy and transferred to the Rothschild hospital and saved from deportation. Several of these Foundation staff members were actually arrested by the authorities, deported and exterminated in the camps. One month before the Liberation of Paris the situation for the Jews had become so dire that my mother, expecting to be arrested at any moment, had given away a load of clothes and furniture to her neighbors. In 1942, my aunt Golda was arrested during a raid on a 4th arrondissement building. She was picked up in the presence of my dumbfounded mother, who was paying her an afternoon visit. My mother wasn't on the list. Was it a twist of fate or her British passport? In any event, she had escaped the death camps once again.

Now that the nightmare was over for her, she was getting her furniture back and the apartment was regaining its normal shape. On the evening of my return home we took a walk around the Place des Vosges. I didn't tell my story, she was more interested in making sure I was eating, sleeping well and doing well. My mother was always ever so caring and generous.

Close to my elementary school, adjacent to Victor Hugo's house, an accordionist was playing and two dozen youngsters were dancing. We too danced. With my US soldier's uniform I made quite an impression in Paris. After strolling on the rue Saint-Antoine we returned home to our chilly apartment: coal and wood were running scarce in Paris. I slept in my childhood bed, which felt strange.

Bernard finally reunited with his mother after six years. Place des Vosges, Paris, September 1944. (Dargols Family Archive)

The next day my mother said, 'Your friend Max, who's in the Forces Françaises Libres and a Gaullist, is on leave and I'm sure he'd like to see you.' He was the son of the hairdresser on the rue de Sévigné. There was hardly any car traffic in Paris owing to the shortage of fuel, but my mother looked at me and said, 'Pay attention when you cross the street', as she fastened my collar so I wouldn't be cold. After all, I had just taken part in the D-day landings...

Leave was soon over. I was then sent to Nice to get some rest for a few days in the Hotel Ruhl, which had been requisitioned by the Americans, after which I went to Bastogne, in Eastern Belgium, where a counter-attack was brewing.

CHAPTER 7

The Ardennes

I arrived in Saint-Vith in early October. We had traded the winding, hedge-lined country roads of Normandy and Brittany for an even more impracticable terrain. Here, the dense forests of pines, the steep hills and abrupt ravines, weren't favorable to our troops. The infantry was in charge of maintaining the front line facing the Siegfried Line of fortifications and obstacles, which ran parallel to the Belgian-German border. For several months, the division held the sector, whose apparent calm was unnerving. We couldn't afford to slacken our vigilance. Heavy rains forced us to move HQs from the muddy forest to Saint-Vith town center and soon the cold and snow would set in. It had already been 120 days since our landing in Omaha Beach and almost a year since boarding the Queen Elizabeth in New York on our way to Scotland.

Shortly after arriving in Saint-Vith, I finally received news from Simon. He was safe and sound, 'somewhere in Southern France.' He had enrolled in the US Army and trained in Florida and Texas for just shy of a year. In June 1944, he'd gotten wind of Operation Overlord. For him and his buddies, the operation seemed to herald the light at the end of the tunnel. Some thought they might not even have to cross the Atlantic. However, I learned much later that Simon had landed in Marseilles on 20 October 1944. He returned as a master corporal and interpreter in the reconnaissance troops of the US 103rd Infantry Division, to the city he'd fled three years earlier to escape the Nazis. He was now 19. Right after landing in Marseilles, and accompanied by two MPs from his unit, he tried to ferret out the man who'd arrested him twice before he left. But the gentleman had run away with his German 'friends'.

My team and I stayed in a large house in Saint-Vith, which had previously been occupied by the Nazis. I surveyed the region in search of new information: in Malmédy, Eupen and Bastogne, where we worked with the *Armée Blanche* (White Army), the Belgian equivalent of the FFI in France.

One October day in 1944, I received a call from an MP informing me that a man named Hans Namuth, in a US uniform, claimed to belong to my team. The MP would detain him

Bernard near Bastogne (Belgium). Winter 1944. (Dargols Family Archive)

until his identity was confirmed. Given Hans' pronounced German accent in French or English, the MP'S concern was legitimate. Added to which the situation in Bastogne was quite tense: rumors of a counter-attack were rife and we learned that some German soldiers had disguised themselves as American military. US soldiers required a password to be recognised by their own unit. Around 150 of these German soldiers, trained by SS Colonel Otto Skorzeny (Mussolini's rescuer) infiltrated units and sabotaged communications. They were masters of imitation: they took on American accents and even our way of opening packs of cigarettes. All of this sowed suspicion within our troops. Some time later, Simon encountered the same problems in Bastogne. He and twelve other troopers, trapped in an ambush, waited until morning to rejoin their unit but didn't know the new password. They had to state their identity at top speed to avoid being shot at by their own side.

To foil the disguised Germans' plan we asked questions only Americans living at the time in the US could answer. We would ask the name of Mickey Mouse's fiancée, Sinatra's given name, the price of a stamp or the name of a baseball player. But in my teammate Hans Namuth's case, given his German accent and origins, this hadn't completely dispelled any doubts.

My phone call didn't do the trick either: with a few well-chosen words, I could pull it off as a New Yorker for a couple of minutes, but the conversation dragged on and before long the MP I was talking to detected foreign inflections in my accent. He decided to keep Hans in custody. In the end, I had to go out to Bastogne with the military accreditation allowing our photographer to be released.

During a 24-hour leave, I went to Brussels with another officer. Other than the Ardennes region, all of Belgium was free. I was given the most amazing welcome. Just a few days away from the front line, I was surprised to see that here the war seemed a thing of the past already. People went to the movies and cafés, they danced and enjoyed popular American songs, such as '*My Heart belongs to Daddy.*'[1] In the evening, soldiers idled arm in arm with young women. I wasn't even allowed to carry my gun on me. The people who spoke English pinned a white star on their lapel, in a gesture of friendliness to the soldiers. After this short spree, returning to France was daunting and my demobilization seemed a very distant future.

Back in the Ardennes, I was sent to Malmédy, some 20 kilometers from Saint-Vith. Rumours of a heavy spy infiltration pervaded the front line. The region was considered a pro-Nazi bastion: the Belgian town of Malmédy was German before 1919. Our team was sent to investigate what was brewing and a sign in very large letters grabbed our attention: *Service de Recrutement pour Volontaire SS.*[21] Our mission was very much hampered by the fact that the majority of people in the town spoke German, while very few spoke French. Despite this, we were able to inform the commanding officer of a German counter-attack in preparation.

A few days later I heard dozens of German tanks arriving, followed by their infantry, but the division was poised for the attack. Together with the 99th Division, the 2nd Division pushed back several German offensives until December 1944. The battle was brutal and there were thousands of casualties, but ultimately the 2nd Division managed to retake Malmédy from the German Army.

A new mission now awaited me in Paris. I was going to be part of the CIC, the Counter Intelligence Corps of the US Army.

Before leaving the position in Belgium, which was so close to Germany, I decided to disobey orders not to go there: I wanted a souvenir photo. I set off on my own in the jeep and stopped before the sign saying *Off limits. You are entering enemy*

In front of an SS recruiting service. Malmédy, Belgium, November 1944.
(Dargols Family Archive)

Bernard entering Germany. November 1944. (Dargols Family Archive)

territory. I carried on towards Aachen, a city well known for manufacturing the best needles for industrial sewing machines, but on the way I became aware of the danger and risks of my little caper into enemy territory, and so I turned back.

CHAPTER 8

Paris: Counter Intelligence Corps

In November 1944, I arrived in Paris for a few months and became an agent of the Counter Intelligence Corps.

The CIC headquarters were housed in the former building of the *Kommandantur*, the Nazi HQ for the Paris region. My office faced the *Opera Garnier*, at the corner of the Avenue de l'Opéra and the rue du Quatre-Septembre. My new team comprised of six agents and our mission was to monitor whatever might harm the men, management and facilities of the US Army in France.

Like me, most of the CIC agents came from the Military Intelligence Service and had also been trained at Camp Ritchie. Many knew one or several foreign languages. Others were law graduates or former policemen. As a CIC agent, I was allowed to wear civilian clothes, which I asked my father to send me. I received a parcel from him: a gray jacket with large shoulder pads, outlining a typical American figure, whereas French fashion favored more fitted clothes. Civilians would have spotted me straight away, so I kept my uniform but stripped it of my stripes and badges to conceal my rank. However, owing to the golden US badge on either side of my shirt collar and cap, it was obvious that I belonged to the US Army. Now, although my US rank hadn't changed, I was called 'sir' instead of 'sergeant'.

I quickly resumed my interrogations of civilians, but this time sitting at a desk. It felt odd to have a desk job after months of rambling across Normandy, Brittany and the Ardennes in my jeep. There, civilians were brought to me by an MP and

Bernard Dargols at the Counter Intelligence Corps headquarters. Place de l'Opéra, Paris, November 1944. (Dargols Family Archive)

the purpose of my questioning was different. At the CIC, I interrogated French civilians who wanted to work for the American forces.

I had more than four pages of ID card numbers of people who were to be arrested on the spot if they happened to come my way. No names were provided. I had to make sure the person I was grilling hadn't collaborated with the Germans. There was always one, or several MPs within reach. Each time someone turned out to be on my list I signalled to an MP, who would proceed to haul him/her off. As for the others, I began with inquiring about their reasons for wanting to work with the Americans, then I would ask trick questions such as 'How long did you work for the Germans? What do you think of Pétain? What papers do you read?' If they answered *Le Pilori, Je suis Partout* or *La Gerbe,*[22] I had them figured out, while they, assuming I was American, had no idea their reading preferences disqualified them without the slightest hesitation.

Pass issued to Bernard Dargols on 4 August 1945 showing that he was a member of the Military Intelligence Service. (Dargols Family Archive)

I investigated Franco-American couples who wanted to get married. I made sure neither potential groom or bride was already married, and that the marriage wasn't meant for the sole purpose of acquiring US citizenship.

I would also look into luxury hotels such as the *Lotti* and the *Meurice,* which German officers had used as dormitories. General von Choltitz, who was appointed military governor of Paris by Hitler in early August 1944, stayed at the *Meurice*. On 23 August, Hitler had ordered him to destroy Paris, its buildings, bridges and roads. Convinced that German defeat was inevitable and hoping to save his skin and ensure himself a less painful future, Choltitz had disobeyed. In both hotels, I set up a large table in the lobby where I summoned all the staff members in turn, from the manager to the maids, to question them about the German occupation and try to identify collaborators. I remember both operations were disappointing, yielding no significant information.

For a short spell I was also called on to work at the American embassy, in the Place de la Concorde. I remember an agent taking me to the basement of the embassy. He offered me coffee and detailed the mission that was going to last for only a few days. I had to sort documents with various levels of confidentiality: from 'Restricted' and 'Confidential', all the way to 'Top secret'. I was proud that my discretion was valued to the point of being entrusted with this mission.

We slept in a small requisitioned hotel on the rue de Helder (in the 9th arrondissement, very close to the *Opera Garnier*), but I often visited my mother and stayed with her overnight. My home town had changed quite a lot: the city was bustling with political activity. On 11 November 1944, I caught sight of Churchill and De Gaulle among an eager crowd on the Place de l'Etoile.

The situation was difficult for Jews returning to Paris. Those whose apartment or business had been confiscated or stolen had to engage in long and tedious procedures to recover their goods and to hire a lawyer. I took advantage of being in Paris to check on the apartment belonging to Françoise's parents. The concierge told me the Germans had taken everything and that a renter still lived there.

Bernard, Place de la Bastille in Paris, October 1945. (Dargols Family Archive)

The people of Paris were delighted that waiting times in stores were shortening, but I was struck by lines longer than 50 meters for the butcher. Living in Paris had become very expensive: sugar, milk, etc., seemed impossible to get by, and ration cards remained indispensable.

French people would frequently show up at the CIC to invite one or several GIs for lunch, to show their gratitude to the US Army for the liberation of France. I recall one invitation I accepted and attended with Toto McCormick, with whom I had been reunited in Paris. In an elegant apartment in Neuilly (an affluent suburb of Paris) we received a warm welcome from the owners of a renowned Champagne establishment.

From the first time we met and during all our missions in Normandy and Brittany, Toto and I had taken to fending off fear with laughter. In that same vein, we decided to pretend not to speak French for the first few moments of the meal in Neuilly, and to show our hosts our true colors shortly after. But the three or four young women at our table made comments concerning our looks. To avoid embarrassing them, we never let them know we spoke French. We had a hard time keeping a straight face.

A few weeks later, on 15 December 1944, all the GIs working in Paris were invited to a Christmas concert to listen to Glenn Miller and his band at the *Café de la Paix*, across the street from the CIC office. As a jazz fan, I couldn't be more thrilled and I got there as soon as I could. We were very excited and looking forward to seeing the band arrive from London any minute, when someone announced that Glenn Miller and his bandmates were late. The plane had been delayed. Unfortunately, after more than an hour waiting, we learned that their plane had disappeared. It had been shot down. We were shocked and very upset. I later learned that Glenn was flown by an inexperienced pilot who had failed to register a flightpath. He had flown under Lancasters who were dumping their bombs above the English Channel in the authorised area, one of which had hit the plane.

I wrote to my father about the tough situation in Paris, which had to remain our priority:

Paris, 17 December 1944

Dear Papa,

The blackout over Paris has been lifted but there isn't that much more light in the streets. There's a shortage of coal to produce electricity. Gas and electricity are available for only a few hours a day. Life is very expensive. A pack of American cigarettes costs between 80 and 100 Francs, whereas for about 45 Francs you can buy a dozen eggs.

Maman has registered to vote. Too many soldiers on the front lines are getting killed, and too many French people are still prisoners in Germany. As a result, the Prefecture has taken a decision, which is rather unpopular for everybody, to prohibit dancing in Paris.

I live in a very kind lady's home and she insists on sending you a note to be read in the States: 'Long Live the Liberators! Long Live America and All Hail to New York! From a French mother, happy to see Allied troops at long last on this good old land that has suffered so much during this long, awful and horrible occupation.'

Bernard

After months on the front, these missions felt much too bureaucratic. I asked to join the parachutists, but I was rejected because my eyesight wasn't good enough. I had no regrets, because I understood that I was much more useful within the anti-terrorist section. American agents who spoke fluent French weren't that common.

***

In March 1945 I was therefore pleased to be sent in the field in Châlons-sur-Marne (nowadays Châlons-en-Champagne) to continue my missions. I was promoted to the rank of Special Agent in Charge. I was in charge of five departments covering roughly the region of Champagne, but excluding the city of Reims, which had been abandoned by most of its inhabitants. We settled in a very large pavilion, previously occupied by the Gestapo. In the pavilion's lounge was a painting by Françoise's great-uncle. It was quite a coincidence: I had met *Oncle* [Uncle] Jules after the liberation of Paris, and could not miss the authorship of the painting that belonged to the owners of the house requisitioned by the Germans. Years later, I visited the owners of the house in Châlons-sur-Marne with Françoise. They told us the painting was given to their daughter by the painter himself, a few years before the war.

The Counter Intelligence Corps team (Bernard is on the far right), Châlons-sur-Marne, November 1945. (Dargols Family Archive)

I received a letter from my brother Marcel:

New York, 31 March 1945

Dear brother,

Tomorrow we'll already be in April. This time around doesn't feel like the beginning of the end, but the end of the end. It's looking good from every point of view... A few days ago I read a very funny article in the Times. *It was about a German soldier captured by the Americans. He was 52. When the Americans interrogated him, asking him what he was doing in the army at his age, he answered, 'I belong to the Hitler Youth!' I wouldn't be surprised if the* Times *article were true. I hope you can go to Paris now and again.*

Give Maman and Grandfather a kiss from me.

Keep well [in English in the text]

Marcel

One of my missions consisted of supervising trains coming from Provence and stopping in Suippes, 20 kilometres from Châlons-sur-Marne. GIs got off the train to relax and we made sure that nothing untoward happened to the convoys before they set off again to go and fight in Germany. As chance had it, one of these convoys was the US 103rd Division, where my younger brother Simon had enrolled.

The 103rd Division, within Patton's 3rd Army, was advancing toward its final destination; Innsbruck. On 27 April 1945 Simon's unit stopped in the suburb of Landsberg (in Bavaria), the birthplace of Nazism,[23] to carry out a reconnaissance mission. Unknown to them, they had arrived in the vicinity of an extermination camp, from which a strong and unspeakable smell emanated. Simon, along with other troopers from his company, opened the gates of the camp and was horrified to discover piles of cadavers: hundreds of men, women, children. Camp guards were running away. Some were shooting. Upon the Americans arrival, the Germans destroyed documents so as to leave no trace of their acts. A prisoner, who had survived by stealing food from the camp kitchens, threw himself on a guard and beat him to death. Simon and the other GIs watched the scene without moving.

Dumbfounded by the sheer horror they were facing, the GIs now understood more than ever the reality of the war they were waging. The landings, the years of training and the hard months of battle that had occurred took on a whole new meaning.

Simon saw three survivors walking in his direction, two of which were wearing the striped camp clothes. One of them, seeing the American soldiers, repeated over and over again, 'Does anyone speak Yiddish?' Simon, who did, answered in Yiddish, and the skeleton-like man embraced and kissed him. Simon recognised himself in them. Along with our father and brother Marcel, he had escaped several arrests before leaving for Cuba, and now understood how lucky he was to be alive. He was haunted by feelings of revenge and hate. He still remembered witnessing our uncle's arrest from the attic room window.

During the few hours he spent in the camp he searched for Uncle Salomon and Aunt Golda among the bodies of the victims. What had happened to them? Were they in this camp or another? Unfortunately, these questions about deported friends and family were unanswerable. But thanks to Serge Klarsfeld's work some years ago, I learned that my Uncle Salomon was part of the 5 June 1942 convoy 2 leaving for Auschwitz. His wife Golda was sent there on 29 July 1942, in convoy 12, which departed from Drancy. At the time they were told they were 'going East'. Both died at Auschwitz.

The 103rd Division forced the local civilians to visit the camps and to give the exterminated prisoners a proper burial: the German civilians who were interrogated said they 'knew nothing', or 'smelled nothing', and no one had 'anything against the Jews'. The unit subsequently liberated three other death camps, that is to say four out of the eleven camps in the Landsberg region.

General 'Ike' Eisenhower visited one of these camps. 'Take a good look around you, because some day, some people will say none of this ever existed.' His speech sounds prophetic today, given the deniers who maintain nothing happened. My brother, myself, and many more can bear witness to the truth. How is it even possible to deny the overwhelming evidence? Fortunately, Ike had the prescience to ask the US Army Signal Corps to document this abominable scene.

Simon was part of the Task Force which left for Innsbruck on the same day to carry out other missions. He would search houses for Nazi weapons and documents, bringing back anti-Semitic pamphlets, weapons and Nazi flags. He was then transferred to the reconnaissance troops of the 45th Division in Munich, and then to the Claims Section in Paris.

A few years ago, Simon set out to find some survivors of the camp his unit had liberated. To that end, he appeared on the French television show *Perdu de Vue*.[24] One survivor, Charles Baron, came forward. They met and a strong friendship ensued. Baron died in March 2017.

For my part, I wasn't yet aware of the extent of the abominations committed by the Nazis.

***

On 13 April 1945, I was in the CIC office in Châlons-sur-Marne sitting at the table and talking with my fellow soldiers when the phone rang. President Roosevelt had died. We were all speechless and deeply saddened. As President and Commander in Chief he was successful in uniting the American people around him and in convincing the isolationist country of the need to help the Allies defeat the Nazi occupiers.

For my twenty-fifth birthday I received a V-Mail dated 28 April 1945, from Marcel in New York:

> *Dear brother,*
>
> *For several weeks now we have been receiving amazing news about the war. The radio and newspapers have announced victory upon victory. It's not going well for the Nazis. In fact, this morning the first photos of the meeting between the first Yanks and some Russian soldiers were published. The fall of Berlin shouldn't be long now, since three-quarters have already been captured. The San Francisco Conference is moving ahead and I hope everything will turn out as well as on the battlefield.[25] Maman's birthday was this week and I hope this V-mail reaches you in time for your 25th birthday. And to think we haven't been able to celebrate your birthday together since 1938! And since we're only getting good news these days, Papa just received his visa and it's possible that you might be seeing each other earlier than you think. Wishing you a happy birthday.*
>
> *Marcel.*

For VE Day on 8 May 1945, McCormick and I were invited to visit the *Champagnes Pol Roger* vineyard in Épernay, close to

Châlons-sur-Marne. The owner gave us a tour of the immense cellars and at every turn we had a little glass of champagne. It became hard to keep my balance and I bumped my head, which prompted me tell Toto that 'at least, I'll be able to say I was wounded at the front [of my head]!'[26]

During the following six months, I continued to monitor the safety of American facilities because the war was still going on in Eastern Europe. McCormick and I were sent to a hospital in Mourmelon, not far from Châlons, a very large facility which was reserved for the American military. We were wearing our special US Army uniform, stripped of ranking badges. A very impressed colonel gave us the full military salute. As mere sergeants, we were more than surprised to be propelled to the top of the hierarchy by the CIC badge and even provided with the power to demote the colonel if our report was unfavorable towards him.

My father obtained a visa for his return to France, but to recover his store, which had been requisitioned for four years, he needed to buy it back. He had to sell the New York store and, back in Paris, asked me to attend the negotiations with the French manager. He thought my uniform might impress him. And so, while on leave, I went to Paris and was reunited with my father after several years of separation. My parents hadn't seen each other for six years. My two grandmothers had passed away during the war, as well as my paternal grandfather. Only my maternal grandfather had survived, despite several months in the internment camp at Drancy. There was much emotion.

We entered the store. The manager, sitting at my father's desk, easily relented, but the store nonetheless had to be bought back. Later, in spite of my dogged efforts, I never managed to track down the two collaborator managers who had robbed my father of his goods. They had fled after the war and I later learned that they were dead.

In December 1945 I was ordered to return to the US from the port of Marseilles. Once back in Virginia, in January 1946, I went to Fort Dix where I was demobilised. My journey had come full circle.

Bernard and his brother Simon photographed in front of a fire department telephone while on leave. Rue de l'Ave-Maria, Paris, end of 1944. (Dargols Family Archive)

CHAPTER 9

Back to Civilian Life

After my demobilization at Fort Dix, I took the train to New York. I was eager to see my brothers again and Françoise even more. Our wedding was celebrated two months later, on 7 April 1946, at the New School for Social Research, where her father worked. Françoise finished her studies and graduated from Columbia University and I was concerned that my father needed my help with the store in Paris.

Returning to the whirlwind of civilian life wasn't that easy. Many GIs had a hard time finding work, while Françoise and I travelled back and forth from New York to Paris by boat several times.

My cousin, David Badache, picked us up in Le Havre where we arrived after our first crossing. A Lithuanian native and an engineer, he was a brilliant man and an ardent supporter of the French republic. He had settled in Caen, where he had set up a paint factory and started a family. But under the Occupation, he was taken hostage by the French police and deported. An Auschwitz survivor, he never talked about his internment and could no longer sleep. I was struck by how extremely skinny he was.

In the 1990s, I accompanied David to Auschwitz. He showed me the gas chambers and cremation ovens, and told me about his death march from the camp. He showed me the barracks where he was locked up. Such horror and unspeakable pain were unbearable. He was among those who, after the war, helped me grapple with the full extent of the Nazi barbarism which we had fought against.

Françoise and Bernard in New York, 1946. (Dargols Family Archive)

A few years went by. We decided to go back to France for good with our two daughters, Lillian and Annie. In Paris our third child, Alain, was born. Life returned to normal: work, children, family, friends, holidays. Besides my categorical refusal to go camping (enough with sleeping in tents already, I'd more than paid my dues!), memories of my GI life were safely tucked away in a corner of my mind: they were still vivid, but I could live with them.

My children were growing up and they would regularly ask me about my life as a soldier. These questions were always unanswered, I stayed mum. I couldn't find the right words to recount the hardship. Those that did come to mind were completely unequal to reality.

Now living on different continents, Thierry McCormick, Hans Namuth, and Eddie Coleman and I remained very close. We didn't need to talk to understand each other. Hans became a photographer, famous worldwide for his photos of Jackson Pollock, among others, and Eddie a golf instructor of some fame in California.

In the 1950s, with the Cold War in full swing, demonstrators marched in the capital with 'US Go Home' signs. I was shocked and hurt. Had the French people already forgotten everything? Had they already forgotten the thousands of young men, fresh in my mind, who had died for them to live free?

Thirty years went by.

In 1984 Eddie Coleman, passing through France, wished to attend the commemorations for the 40th anniversary of the D-Day landings. For both of us former GIs, this began with us writing a very short letter relating our story, which is how my family discovered what I'd never managed to tell them before.

On Omaha Beach our memory was revived, and our emotion was great. As I rediscovered the fine sandy beach, so large, so beautiful, the sound of guns, the smell of death and the fear were still very much in my mind. Facing the monument erected in memory of the 2nd Division, I thought how lucky I was to be alive. The French author Jérôme Garcin describes the beach so well:

In Saint-Laurent-sur-Mer, in the harsh Bessin, the landing beach's wilderness, peopled with young ghosts, bordered by sad dunes, capped with blockhouses, swept by gray winds, hardly frequented, grooved by the chains of amphibious boats, studded with sharp-edged carcasses, rusted metal sheets and indeterminate metals which time tore off the Allied armada, is now the open-air sanctuary of D-Day, where multi-colored tourists parade.[27]

I was surprised to discover that some people collect objects pertaining to the Landing. During the commemorations, others might dress as GIs, or drive jeeps, all contributing to preserving the memory of these events. At that point, I handed over my revolver, which I'd kept in some corner, as well as my helmet. What had I done with my uniform? I don't know, I only held on to the most important items: my division's badge, my double dog-tag stamped with my service number, the bracelet Françoise gave me before I joined the army, and above all, the memory of those who, unlike me, were not lucky enough to survive.

In fact, this good luck has haunted me throughout my whole life. Why me and not them? Was it fate, or a lucky star watching over me? Incredible and burdensome luck, to which I remain forever beholden. After the war, some of my friends started believing in God whom they thought had protected them, while others, believing their faith had failed them, abandoned it for good. My memory is still vivid: flashbacks of combat keep on preventing me from falling asleep, fireworks bring me back to the horrifying sound of bombings. My war recollections cannot be erased.

The names of the villages we liberated are etched in my mind: Formigny, Trévières, St Georges d'Elle, Cerisy-la-Forêt, Bérigny, among others.

With some heartache, I retrod the path of the Landing, this time with my family and friends. I explained how seventy-three years ago, the beach was covered with soldiers about to enter France, where they would move up to the front line, but for many of them, where they would lose their life. Today, the memory of these men is embedded in dozens of headstones, museums, places of remembrance, these 'objects that escape oblivion'.[28]

One such monument, the 'Les Braves' sculpture, set in the sands of Omaha Beach, symbolises the first wave of GIs. Like the beach-bound statue, these GIs, who were killed in the water or on the beach's sands, were prevented from ever setting foot on French soil.

Invited to the commemorations by mayors, department or state representatives, I was very moved by the words of praise. I received medals I never asked for, but which I symbolically shared with all the men from my division, 'my Indianhead comrades whose twenty-years sleep, forever and today, facing the Sea of Normandy.'[29]

Statue of 'Les Braves', Saint-Laurent-sur-Mer, 2010. (Dargols Family Archive)

CHAPTER 10

Never Again

'Life is like a play: it's not the length, but the excellence of the acting that matters.' Seneca

Seventy-three years have passed. I am fairly well-seasoned, but not wise enough to show at least some tolerance for yesterday's enemy: Nazi dictatorship and inhumanity, the execrable ideology which some supported and carried out with determination. Unlike the Napoleonic Wars or the First World War, this war caused more civilian than military deaths.

Today, at ninety-seven years of age, I still can't understand why educated people perpetrated crimes in such organised ways, how they came to kill men, women and children on the grounds of religion, among other reasons. How can a man shoot a woman and child in the back? Or let them die of hunger, or exterminate them in such methodical ways? How could decimating Jews be the sole purpose of the *Einsatzgruppen*,[30] these task forces composed of volunteers from the educated classes of an advanced country? Paragons of knowledge proved themselves capable of the worst crimes. But aren't culture and education supposed to ward off and undermine extremist ideologies? Evidently not. Relentless and sustained vigilance is of vital importance.

Without necessarily belonging to a political party, remaining capable of outrage and action is essential when confronted with extremist speeches or racists words, or when a town wants to name a public school after a journalist and proven collaborationist, as was the case in La Garenne-Colombes, a Parisian suburb, in 2009. A protest group was created, which

Bernard in Saint-Laurent-sur-Mer, Omaha Beach, 2008. (Dargols Family Archive)

I joined. At its head was Marc Schindler, a man who battled determinedly for several months until the town gave in and dropped the name Kléber Haedens. Likewise in Saint-Cloud, another suburb of Paris, a high-school's name was changed in 2004 after forty years of bearing the name of a pro-Nazi composer, Florent Schmitt.

In spite of my unshakable optimism, I remain sceptical: how can a repetition of these tragic events be foiled? What can be done against the people who seek to rewrite history? How can the narratives that minimise facts to the point of blotting them out be countered?

Because, although more people continue to bear witness, historical negationism is also on the rise.

***

Bernard back in Cerisy-la-forêt in Normandy for the 50th anniversary of D-Day (1994), in front of a jeep closely resembling La Bastille. (Dargols Family Archive)

For the 50th anniversary of D-Day, I read a very moving letter from René Garrec, President of the Lower Normandy Regional Council, to his grandson:

> *Dear Adrien,*
>
> *I watch you playing with your brothers, and it brings back to me the distress I felt when, one by one, the war picked off several members of my family. Thank God you don't know yet that fifty years on, you still miss someone who was dear to you. May you never know…*
>
> *The veterans who will be coming here are now seventy years of age or more; you will probably look on them as being very distant people. Yet you've got to understand that if you live in a free country today, you owe it to them. They came from a long way, and they were terribly young, to fight against a dreadful regime that had enslaved Europe and killed thousands of children your age, whose only crime had been to be born to parents whose religion was different from the religion of most French people. (…) I hope all parents will make the effort to explain to their children what was done for us. Then they will know that they did not fight for nothing. They will also know, and this is also vital for them, that their comrades, whose bodies are buried along our shores, did not die in vain. (…)*
>
> *We must remember them all, Adrien, and maybe the last ones most of all. (…) Doubtless they will sleep better if little boys of your age spare a thought for them now and then.*

I wrote to René Garrec, also speaking to his grandson:

> *Dear Adrien,*
>
> *Do you know that you are really lucky to have a grandfather like yours, who is already trying to make you understand the meaning of those two words; Freedom and Democracy? When a dictatorship tries to do away with*

them, there comes a time when they are worth fighting for, and even dying for. War is a sad business, you know. I didn't like it either, because when you're twenty years old, there are things much more fun to do; but I am happy to have fought so that we may all have peace – you, your parents, your grandparents and, one day, your own children as well. True, we didn't fully succeed, but if we had lost, I'm sure life wouldn't have been worth living.

Your grandfather made one mistake in his article: of all of my army comrades now living in New York, in California and North Carolina, neither they nor I ever looked upon ourselves as being 'heroes'. The heroes are lying in the cemeteries at Omaha Beach and the surrounding region.

You may be a strong soldier with a helmet, a sub-machine gun and a pistol, but I can assure you that a soldier cries as well. And I want you to cry tears of joy every time you feel you want to cry.

And yet after my time as a soldier I had other reasons to cry - reasons that awoke the very feelings that I'd kept deeply buried for a long time. Feelings of anger and injustice. This is what I felt learning about my daughter Annie's multiple sclerosis, which she fought against for most of her life with so much strength and courage. And again those feelings hit me when my grand-daughter, Caroline, lost her husband Christophe during a gig at the Bataclan concert hall on 13 November 2015, in the Paris terrorist attacks which left their 2-year-old and 6-year-old children fatherless, as well as 130 other young lives that were brutally stolen. Whether at the Bataclan listening to music, on the surroundings bar terraces having a good time, or at the Stade de France where a soccer game was taking place, people were killed because they were celebrating normal life. And so many other events worldwide left me powerless. Wars, genocides and recent terrorist attacks in Europe and the rest of the world: Madrid, Nice, Brussels, London, Manchester, Abidjan, St Petersburg, Stockholm, Barcelona... This new war against freedom and democracy must be fought with the tools of democracy.

I would still like to be assured that the crimes we fought against will never occur again.

***

I try to visit elementary, middle and high schools as often as possible and am always invited there by teachers, intent on having their students meet witnesses of the wars they study. I am convinced that it is important to tell children the story of wars for them to fully understand why they need to protect peace, or, in the words of Simone Veil:

> *Today's young people must know how those who, more than fifty years ago, were their age and lived the joys and sorrows of an ordinary child or adolescent, were thrust into violence, horror, madness and hatred. They must know how, barely twenty years after the first war, which had killed entire generations of young men, the world was again driven to another global conflict even more deadly... We know - and the news reminds us - that History is never irreversible. The commemoration of the landing in Normandy leads us to measure how much progress we've made on the way towards peace between our countries, and encourages us to unite even more.*[31]

I hand over the duty to be watchful to today's youth. Dictatorship, like an invasive and poisonous weed, can be eradicated if it's nipped in the bud: extremist ideas cannot be allowed to thrive. The recent elections worldwide, whether in the USA or in Europe, should alert us to the urgent need to resist the messages of fear and hatred that divide people. Voting remains one of our strongest weapons, of which we have to be sure it is used wisely.

During a commemoration, I met an English teacher in Sainte-Foye-la-Grande, near Bordeaux. Christelle Zuccolotto is determined to enshrine the memory of those who fought Nazism. This has become an educational project for which, year after year, she toils to gather funding: after working on the subject of the landing with her students and their History and French teachers, she takes around fifty of them to the beaches of Normandy. Their questions might sometimes sound unexpected, for instance 'Were the GIs doped before landing?' But no, aside from the dishwater (coffee), of which we drank loads, no doping!

In Normandy, I'm surprised by the amount of people intent on keeping history alive. The former mayor of Saint-Laurent-sur-Mer, Raymond Mouquet, is such a person who, with others, has turned his small village into a forward-looking place of remembrance. Each year he warmly welcomes young Americans, 'Student Ambassadors' from the *People to People* organization,[32] who come to Normandy to walk in the footsteps of the veterans, often a family member. It's also the case with Ken Forder, former US consul in Bordeaux, who contributed so much to the Franco-American friendship. Other groups too are devoted to remembering: *France Will Never Forget, Les Liens de l'Histoire, Libertyship Overlord, D-Day Overlord, Omaha Beach Bedford, Les Fleurs de Mémoire* (which puts flowers on the tombs of the GIs who fell during the Second World War), the Second Indianhead Division Association, as well as prefects, mayors or house representatives such as Jean-Paul Garraud, Jean-Pierre Richard, Jocelyne Le Trouit, to name a few, who have organised conferences and commemorations in memory of the Liberation.

Winston Churchill once said that, 'A nation that forgets its past has no future'. It is of utmost importance for me to pay tribute to all these men and women who've become my friends, and to all the others who fight against oblivion.

***

Twenty major worldwide leaders including Queen Elizabeth, Presidents Obama and Hollande and Chancellor Merkel gathered in Normandy for D-Day's 70th Anniversary commemorations and to pay tribute to the veterans, of which the numbers are dwindling. During a ceremony, I discovered I was sitting next to a veteran medic of my division, Oscar Peterson, who had travelled from Washington State to Normandy with his wife, children and grandchildren. We had landed on Omaha Beach on the same day. We might have talked to each other or walked side by side on 8 June 1944, but we didn't recall. However, the emotion was huge between us and our families. I can foresee the day when all of us will have passed away. There might then be people, politicians or academics even, who would have the nerve to profess that Operation Overlord was just a Hollywood movie. We run the risk that those who today deny the existence of the concentration camps, death camps and incineration ovens, later contend that nothing ever happened. Do not believe these people, they're living proof that one can be at once educated and ruthless, capable of lying, torturing and even killing for their ideas.

I encourage them to visit Omaha Beach, where they would find one of these immense military cemeteries, the Coleville cemetery, with its manicured lawn and row upon row of 10,000 impeccably aligned tombs. All but a few cover the bodies of young Americans who perished in the Omaha sector during the longest week of my life, and the shortest of theirs. The week of 6 June 1944.

When my five great-grandchildren, the eldest of which is 11, are old enough to wonder about the Second World War, they, too might ask themselves if the camps, the gas chambers, the Landing in Normandy really existed.

This book will remind them that these events did occur. The Landing wasn't just a show: I was there.

Glossary

Ausweiss: authorization delivered by the Germans, permitting the crossing of the Demarcation Line between free and occupied France.

AWOL: Absent Without Leave

CIC: Counter Intelligence Corps

DCA: Defense against Aircrafts

Double dog-tag: a GI's double Identification tag

Einsatzgruppen: mobile death squads

KP: Kitchen Police (potato peeling duty)

GI: Government Issued

Fox-hole: a small hole dug by a soldier at each stop to protect himself from bombings.

HICEM: the result of the merger of three Jewish migration associations in 1927: New York-based HIAS (Hebrew Immigrant Aid Society); Jewish Colonization Association (JCA); and Emigdirect (United Jewish Emigration Committee), a migration organization based in Berlin.

IPW: Interrogation of Prisoners of War

LCVP: Landing Craft Vehicle & Personnel

Liberty ships: troop ships about 440 ft long

LICA: acronym for *Ligue Internationale Contre l'Antisémitisme* [International League Against anti-Semitism], today it is known as LICRA.

Medic: US Medical officer

MII: US Military Intelligence Interpreter

MIS : US Military Intelligence Service

MP: Military Police

Ordnance: US Army unit in charge of military vehicle maintenance

Panzer division: German Army armored (tank) division

PI: Photograph Interpreter

Private: a soldier of the lowest military rank

U-boat: anglicised version of the German word U-Boot, a shortening of *Unterseeboot*, literally 'undersea boat' (submarine)

Signal Corps: US Army corps responsible for military communications, including photographs and movies

STO: acronym for *Service de Travail Obligatoire,* Compulsory Work Service, carried out by French men in Germany

Stuka: Abbreviation of the German word *SturzKampfflugzeug,* 'dive bomber'

V1 and V2: German flying bombs

VE-Day: Victory in Europe Day, the day of the Germans' defeat and of the liberation of France, on 8 May 1945

V-mail: Victory mail, letter reduction process used by the US Army during the Second World War

WAC: US Women's Army Corps

Bibliography

Combat History of the Second Infantry Division in World War II, (Baton Rouge, Army and Navy Publishing Co.), 1946

Basse Normandie Magazine. N°17, June 1994

Besnaci-Lancou, Fatima, Benoit Falaize, and Gilles Manceron, eds., *Les Harkis, Histoire, Mémoire et Transmission*, (Editions de l'Atelier), 2010

Blond, Georges, *Le Débarquement,* (Editions Presses de la Cité), 1984

Borlant, Henri, *Merci d'avoir survécu*, (Paris, Editions du Seuil), 2001

Deuve, Jean, *Histoire Secrètes des Stratagèmes de la Seconde Guerre Mondiale - Duperies, Tromperies, Intoxications, Illusions de 1939 à 1945*, (Paris, Nouveau Monde Éditions), 2008

Garcin, Jérôme, *Olivier*, (Paris, Éditions Gallimard), 2011

Guéno, Jean-Pierre, ed., *Paroles du Jour J, Lettres et Carnets du Débarquement, Été 1944*, (Paris, Éditions Librio), 2004

Laub, Dori. 'Bearing witness' in Shoshana Felman and Dori Laub eds., *Testimony: Crises of Witnessing in Literature, Psychoanalysis and History*, (New York and London, Routledge), 1992

Patrick, Ian, *Héros Anonymes, Portraits Par Ian Patrick*, (Editions Ian Duncan Patrick), 2009

Thiébot, Emmanuel. *Chroniques de la Vie des Français sous l'Occupation.* Paris: Éditions Larousse, 2011

Waintrater, Régine, *Sortir du Génocide, Témoigner Pour Apprendre à Vivre*, (Paris, Éditions Payot), 2003

Wiesel, Elie, *Night*, (Hill & Wang Inc., U.S.), 2006

Filmography

The Ritchie Boys, Dir. Christian Bauer, 2004

Why We Fight, Dir. Frank Capra, 1942–1945

Apocalypse, the Second World War, Dir. Isabelle Clarke and Daniel Costelle, 2009

From Earth to Moon, Dir. Tom Hanks, 1995

Europa, Europa, Dir. Agnieszka Holland, 1990

 Shoah, Dir. Claude Lanzmann, 1985

Train of Life [Train de vie], Dir. Radu Mihaileanu, 1998

Night and Fog [Nuit et Brouillard], Dir. Alain Resnais, 1955

From Nuremberg to Nuremberg [De Nuremberg à Nuremberg], Dir. Frédéric Rossif, 1994

Band of Brothers, Dir. *Steven Spielberg,* 2001

Saving Private Ryan, Dir. Steven Spielberg, 1998

Schindler's List, Dir. Steven Spielberg, 1993

The Battleground, Dir. William Wellman, 1950

The Longest Day, Dir. Darryl F. Zanuck, 1962

Acknowledgements

Thanks to my late husband Christophe Foultier, who taught me how to make my dreams come true and whom we miss every single day.

Thanks to my grandparents Françoise and Bernard, who opened their hearts and memories and answered thousands of questions. Thanks to my mother Lillian for spending too many hours re-reading and editing my notes, and thanks to both of my parents for always believing that I was capable of completing this work.

Thanks to Simon and Marcel Dargols and Annie Dargols Grasso, who I wish I could share this book with.

Thanks to Charlie Badache, Isabelle Bournier, and my publishers Matthieu Biberon at Ouest France, and Heather Williams at Pen and Sword Books for their trust and help.

A special thanks to Françoise Rudetzki, Asma Guenifi and Dr Laurent Bernard-Brunel who have helped me so much through this journey.

Thanks to Isabelle Kite for translating the text with so much talent and enthusiasm.

Thanks to Michel Labro, Nathalie Collin, Louis Dreyfus, Marine Mercier and Rudy Fagnaud, Laetitia Marisa and Christophe Stenström, Adeline and Mark Townsley, Claire and Olivier Magnana, Annie and Bernard Foultier, Flore Sionneau, Chloé Thomas, Stéphanie and Alain Germond, Julie Elmoznino, Romain and Amélie Jolivet, Alain Dargols, Lou Giulianelli, Jennifer and Brad Cherney, Elaine Clayman, Ron Tepperman, Sandra Améziane, Aurélie Sadoine, Nicolas and Agnieszka Chauvel, Bérangère Capdet, Anna Rousseau, Raymond and Nicole Mouquet for their support.

Thanks to Eddie Vedder and Thom Yorke for the inspiration.

For maps, interviews and press releases, please visit www.bernard-dargols.com

Endnotes

1 Régine Waintrater explains the relationship between the witness and the person who records the account in *Sortir du génocide, Témoigner pour apprendre à vivre.* (Paris, Editions Payot, 2003).
2 D. Laub, 'Bearing Witness', in Soshana Felman Shoshana Felman and Dori Laub eds., *Testimony: Crises of Witnessing in Literature, Psychoanalysis and History*, (New York and London, Routledge, 1992), p.70.
3 Wiesel's clsoing words for the 'Rendez-vous de l'histoire' conference (1998), during which *Le Crime et le Pouvoir* and *Train de Vie* by Radu Mihaileanu, were introduced. The latter tells the story of a small village in central Europe in 1941, whose inhabitants organized decoy deportation trains in order to escape the Nazis and head for Palestine.
4 In a radio broadcast delivered on 29 December 1940
5 *Ligue Internationale contre l'Antisémitisme* [International League against anti-Semitism]. The acronym LICRA is today a household name.
6 J. Deuve, *Histoire Secrète des Stratagèmes de la Seconde Guerre Mondiale - Duperies, Tromperies, Intoxications, Illusions de 1939 à 1945.* (Paris, Nouveau monde éditions, 2008). Jean Deuve was an officer specializing in intelligence during the Second World War.
7 An infantry division comprised of approximately 13,000 men.
8 François Darlan was the head of the French collaborationist Vichy government from February 1941. Jacques Doirot was the founder of the *Parti Populaire Français* [French People's Party] in 1936 and wartime collaborator.
9 Compulsory Work Service [*Service de Travail Obligatoire,* STO] carried out by French men in Germany.
10 Defensive counter air: defensive measures designed to detect, identify, intercept, and destroy or negate enemy forces.
11 From Franklin D. Roosevelt's first inaugural address, given on 4 March 1933.
12 Historians estimate the armada bound for Normandy at more than 6,000 ships.

13   E. Pyle, *Paroles du Jour J, Lettres et Carnets du Débarquement, Été 1944*, ed. Jean-Pierre Guéno, (Paris, Editions Librio, 2004).

14   Tranquilizers.

15   Anise-flavored spirit popular in France.

16   On 10 June 1944, the 2nd Waffen-SS Panzer Division 'Das Reich' carried out a massacre in the village of Oradour-sur-Glane, near Limoges. A total of 642 inhabitants were killed, including men, women and children, leaving few survivors. The entire village was destroyed and the ruins have been left as a memorial.

17   V-mail, short for Victory Mail, was a hybrid mail process used by the Americans during the Second World War as the primary and secure method to correspond with soldiers stationed abroad. To reduce the cost of transferring an original letter through the military postal system, V-mail correspondence was carried out on small letter paper, 17.8 cm x 23.2 cm, that would pass through the mail censors before being photographed and transported as a thumbnail-sized image in negative microfilm. Upon arrival at their destination, the negatives would be blown up to 60 percent of their original size, 10.7 cm x 13.2 cm, and printed.

18   TSF (*Télégraphie Sans Fil*: Wireless Telegraph.

19   The United Service Organizations (USO Show) was a non-profit organization founded in 1941 to provide morale to GIs through entertainment.

20   *Forces Françaises de l'intérieur*: French Forces of the Interior (French Resistance).

21   Volunteer SS Recruitment Service.

22   Notoriously collaborationist newspapers.

23   It was in Landsberg prison that Hitler dictated his memoirs (*Mein Kampf*) to Rudolf Hesse, in 1924.

24   A TV programme whose objective was to reunite long-lost friends.

25   The San Francisco Conference was held on 25-26 June 1946 and was attended by delegations from forty-six nations. It resulted in the creation of the United Nations charter.

26   In French: '*au moins je pourrais dire que j'ai été blessé au front!*'

27   J. Garcin, *Olivier,* (Paris, Éditions Gallimard, 2011).

28   P. Nora, in 'Les Harkis, Histoire, Mémoire et Transmission', ed. Fatima Besnaci-Lancou, Benoit Falaize and Gilles Manceron, (Paris, Editions de l'Atelier, 2010).

29   From a poem by Jean Goujon, 2009.

30   Nazi paramilitary death squads.

31   Simone Veil was a camp survivor and a widely-respected French politician. She died in June 2017.

32 The association was born of President Eisenhower's wish to strengthen the brotherhood between civilizations, in order to avoid another conflict. The idea was to eliminate mutual prejudice and have members of these civilizations meet, which is why he asked around 100 personalities, such as Walt Disney, Norman Rockwell and Jesse Owens, to create the People to People program, whose purpose would be to allow ordinary American citizens to meet their counterparts in other countries.

Index